FELIPE ANGELES

AND THE MEXICAN REVOLUTION

SHARON EGGER HESTON

Primix Publishing
East Brunswick Office Evolution
1 Tower Center Boulevard, Ste 1510
East Brunswick, NJ 08816
www.primixpublishing.com
Phone: 1-800-538-5788

Published by Primix Publishing: 02/28/2026

ISBN: 979-8-89194-617-0(sc)
ISBN: 979-8-89194-618-7(e)

Library of Congress Control Number: 2026902018

for Adam and Max.

ACKNOWLEDGEMENTS

During fifteen years of research of the Mexican Revolution many helpful people have crossed my path and generously assisted. My forever friend Doloris Huerta Lloyd joined me exploring the missing decade of my grandfather's life that resulted in our book "Crossing the Line." It was our trips to Douglas, Arizona and Alamos, Mexico; that introduced me to the tragic yet inspiring life of General Felípe Ángeles.

At Claremont College I discovered and translated the archived letters of Governor Jose Maria Maytorena, and his friend General Ángeles. Those bi-weekly letters bring to life events and people who were active in the revolt against Victoriano Huerta.

Visits to El Paso led me to the El Paso Public Library and Claudia Ramirez who freely provided all the newspaper accounts that mentioned Felípe Ángeles. In a later trip I met Claudia Rivers at the University of Texas library where the extensive Borderlands Collection is so generously provided to researchers.

In Las Cruces, New Mexico the University of New Mexico librarian Gracie Garza provided me copies of two archived diaries: one written by Felípe Ángeles himself and the other by Federico Cervantes of the Battle of Zacatecas. I translated and published both diaries in 2014.

In Zacatecas, Mexico at the Historical Archives of the State of Zacatecas, Director Maria Eugenia Maldonado, not only provided written material and photographs of the Battle of Zacatecas but gave a guided tour of the battlefield. There are no words sufficient to express my gratitude to her and to her husband for their generous gift of time and knowledge.

The person most deserving of gratitude is my husband Leonard who encouraged, proofread, chauffeured and made possible all these adventures.

TABLE OF CONTENTS

HISTORICAL TIMELINE

February 18, 1913.

A cabal within the federal army of Mexico arrests and jails elected President Madero.

February 22, 1913.

President Madero and vice President Pino Suarez are assassinated, and General Huerta declares himself president.

March 1913.

The U.S. declares itself against Huerta.

April 1913

Venustiano Carranza, governor of Coahuila, is declared First Chief to fight against Huerta. Three divisions are established; one led by Alvaro Obregon, another by Pablo Gonzalez, and the third, the Northern Division, led by General Francisco Villa.

April 1914

General Felípe Ángeles serves under General Villa as general
of artillery to support the Northern Division.

June 23, 1914.

The Division del Norte (Northern Division) captures the city of
Zacatecas.

July 15, 1914.

Huerta resigns as President of Mexico and flees to the United
States where he is arrested for conspiracy and
held at Fort Bliss. He was released for health
reasons and died of alcoholism in January of
1915.

PREFACE

By 1920, when what Anita Brenner called 'The Wind that Swept Mexico" had passed,[1] it left twenty percent of the population of Mexico dead. Thousands were killed in the fighting, or as innocent bystanders; thousands more died of disease or starvation brought on by the uncertainties of war. The final tragedy was the loss of a generation of leadership. Most of the leaders of the revolution died young and violently.

Streets of Mexico City are named for Heroes of the Mexican Revolution. Villages carry their names as well, but who they were or why they are called heroes is forgotten. An intentional amnesia befell the survivors of the decade of bloodletting.

The revolutionaries succeeded in unseating the dictator Porfirio Diaz only to fall into the hands of a much less benign dictator, General Victoriano Huerta. Then, after driving Huerta out, the victorious revolutionaries began to devour one another in civil war. Finally, on November 26,1919 General Felípe Ángeles was executed by firing squad. With his death all pretense of idealism and dignity were gone. The nation was exhausted; the wind of revolution passed leaving misery, regret and the desire to forget.

CHAPTER ONE

Early Days

Tncided with the modern history of Mexico.[2] He was born in1869, one year after the establishment of the republic and died in 1919, one year before the beginning of the Sonoran Dynasty.[3] He joined a comfortably well-off family of Col. Felípe Ángeles and Juana Ramirez. His father, also named Felípe Ángeles, served Mexico during the Mexican American war of 1847 and again twenty years later in 1867 to restore the Republic from the French intervention with Emperor Maximillian.[4] Felípe Sr. served under the command of General Manuel Mondragon. While serving his country he was wounded twice, once in the head and once in the arm. He refused a pension because he said he served for duty not for money. Before his retirement he achieved the rank of colonel and later became the political chief of several cities in Hidalgo: Zacualtipan, Molongo, Ixmequilpan, Altonilco Grande, Huejutla and Jocala. Later, he became the administrator of *rentas de la aduana,* (customs tax) in Zacualtipan. That was a peaceful time; he was well-liked, and he kept the area quiet and orderly with a light touch.

The indigenous population of the area he controlled was almost entirely illiterate. The spoken languages of the area were Olmec and Nahuatl with Spanish as a little used second language.

Those few who were able to read learned their first letters from private tutors, as did young Felípe, whose tutor was Arcadio Castro, "a man of wisdom who inspired his pupils" said Felípe himself in later writings. When he had learned to read and write and was old enough, he was enrolled in the Literary Institute at Pachuca and studied under the tutelage of Arnaldo Laroule.[5]

Felípe Jesus Ángeles Ramirez was born on June 13, 1869 in the town of Zacualtipan. He was third of four sons to a second marriage. Because of his father's work, he lived in several towns in the valley that runs from Atonilco to Zacualtipan.[6] He grew up in military traditions at the side of the man who exercised political authority. He attended elementary school in Pachuca and finished the required courses by 1883 at the age of fourteen. His father and his teachers could see that schools in the provinces were no challenge for him and Felípe was fortunate that his father was able to do something about it. As a colonel and a government official in good standing he was able to send his son to the Military College at Chapultepec in Mexico City at the exceptionally early age of fourteen.

Felípe was fortunate in another way. In earlier years The Military School was not exceptional in the world of military schools. However, President Porfirio Diaz was determined to build a modern, professional army and the school was undergoing rapid improvements. By1883, admission requirements were high: an applicant must bring a certificate of good conduct and character. He must never have been expelled from any school and must pass entrance exams in arithmetic, algebra, Spanish and beginning French. And he must be between sixteen and eighteen years of age. Felípe demonstrated excellence in mathematics and had glowing recommendations from previous teachers. An age exception could be made to allow a fifteen-year-old to enter if they were a son of an officer. It was by stretching that exception that Felípe was allowed to take the tests; however, his outstanding test results convinced General Sostenes Roca, the school's director, and vice director General Juan Villegas, to allow him to enroll.

It is interesting and a credit to the much-maligned President Porfirio Diaz that he named General Sostenes Rocha director of the school. This was the same General Sostenes Rocha that defeated Diaz when Diaz revolted against Juarez in 1871. Diaz demonstrated pragmatic wisdom and lack of rancor by naming General Sostenes Rocha to be director of the school with the goal of building his professional army

Felípe Ángeles graduated with honors in 1892. There was never a question that he was admitted improperly; he was a perfect fit for the Military School at Chapultepec. His technical skills and successes did not hinder his popularity. He was a good-looking boy and taller than average. He loved sports, fencing, wrestling, and track events but especially horseback riding. He was described as always having a smile. In 1892 when he graduated, he achieved the rank of lieutenant and was commissioned into the battalion of *zapadores,* soldiers who were dedicated to the construction of dams and bridges. Once enrolled, young Felípe moved rapidly through the grades. His record shows that within two years from his enrollment, he rose to Corporal and in another two years he became Sergeant. And in 1890, even before he received the level of lieutenant of engineers, he was designated to teach (without remuneration) the class of Mechanical Analytics. Many of Chapultepec's graduates left the services after graduation to take high paying work in nonmilitary institutions but Ángeles continued the course and was assigned to the Zapadores Battalion. Over the following two-year period he directed the planning and excavation of the canal on the Duero River in Michoacán.

The years between 1898 and 1905 were full: Captain Ángeles wrote a two-volume text entitled; *Formulario de las Velocidades y Presiones en las armas de fuego.* He taught Exterior Ballistics at the Military College. He also taught Theory and Practice of Firing at the Military at the School of Aspirants in Tlalpan.

In September 1901 Captain Ángeles was commissioned to inspect the 75.mm artillery which Mexico had acquired from France. He did not limit himself to a formality. He became chief of the technical group organized by Creusot, the French company that had charge of the development of the gun. This group worked on the hydraulic brakes and the spring recovery mechanism which so improved the Schnieder-Canet canon that military historians have given it prime credit for winning World War I for France and her allies. At least one writer gives Ángeles the major credit.

In August of 1904 his expertise was called upon to evaluate a new invention. He was assigned to accompany General Davila to the United States to evaluate and possibly purchase the new smokeless powder which inventor Hudson Maxim offered to the Mexican army and which General Roselino Martinez had agreed to accept. The group from Mexico was given a tour of the facilities and a demonstration of the explosive. Following the tour an official banquet was held at Lake Hopatcong in New Jersey. At the dinner the senior procurement officer and politician, Rosenda Pineda, praised Maxim and his new product which he said, "would be of great benefit to the Mexican army." But before the affair broke up, Ángeles told the inventor and his group that the powder had not been adequately tested and after two further conferences, Ángeles prevailed, and no contract was made. Maxim was so impressed with Ángeles scientific attitude and willingness to stand up to political pressure that years later when there was a similar question, the inventor recalled that from what he knew of Ángeles character whichever side Ángeles chose was the right one.

Once he returned to Chapultepec a career of teaching developed. From the time of his reception as an engineer and his rise to 2nd Captain, in 1894, Ángeles was Professor of Mathematics.

Ángeles taught classes at both military schools. He rode the trolley from Chapultepec to teach classes at the School of Aspirants in Tlalpan. A fellow passenger caught his eye, a lovely young woman who always got off the trolley at a corner in Tlalpan near the American School. The handsome young officer soon learned she was an American from California. Her mother, Carmen Sanchez was Mexican and her father Carlos Emilio Krause, German. Clara Krause was drawn to Mexico by her maternal heritage. She taught at the American School. Their trolley rides together became a romance and soon the two were married. Their first son, Alberto, was born in 1897. Isabel came next and then in 1903 the twins, Felípe and Julio were born.

The literacy rate in Mexico was such that few youths could pass Chapultepec's entrance exams. The Military School at Chapultepec was established in 1823 and was considered Mexico's West Point. Because there was a was a desperate need for line officers, Felípe Ángeles and likeminded men from the school at Chapultepec founded the new school at Tlalpan in 1901. The school was designed to have lower entrance requirements. It was called the School of Aspirants, or neophytes. The founders, Miguel Rurales, Jose Alessio Robles, Emiliano Lopez, Angel Vallejo and Felípe Ángeles did not want to dilute the quality of graduates from Chapultepec by lowering standards, so they planned the school at Tlalpan to graduate officers more quickly with fewer years of training. Indeed, more officers were graduated, but there was an unintended consequence. Officers from the old Diaz regime, uncultured and relatively incompetent, were registering their ill-prepared sons into the school at Tlalpan and then proclaiming that it provided an education equal to the Military School at Chapultepec. That false claim distressed Felípe Ángeles; it gnawed at him.

His opportunity to make his opinion known arrived in 1905 when he was designated by Director Juan Villegas, to be the orator at the Awards Ceremony. Each year this ceremony was held at the Military College. Traditionally the banquet was attended by President Porfirio Diaz and his six generals (average age seventy-two). Ángeles gave a passionate speech on the subject of improving the school. His speech was completely factual but lacked political finesse and tact.

He stated that what the Aspirants learned in three semesters was what cadets at Chapultepec learned during an after-dinner speech. In his speech he pointed out that the army was weakened by corruption and deceit. And he criticized the six old generals who had been with the president for thirty years and suggested it was time for their retirement. Of course, the generals were furious; so furious they put Ángeles under military arrest. The generals had glorious reputations and chests full of medals to prove it, but were actually ignorant and inept—powerful, but corrupt. They demanded that President Diaz punish Ángeles. However, President Diaz downplayed the arrest. He recognized the potential of his brash young officer and told his old comrades-in-arms that Ángeles was right and instead of punishing Ángeles he sent him to France. Ángeles was out of the way, but the generals were not retired, Such honorable exile was a common tactic used by the military to remove annoying officers. Diaz had another motive. His vision for Mexico included a modern army. He saw that Ángeles had qualities needed to build that army.[7]

Ángeles found the French military academy of St. Cyr exhilarating, full of new ideas and new horizons. The French army was proud and well-equipped. It was the foremost army in Europe at the time and Felípe saw first-hand what a military school could be; The school's motto "Duty, Honor, Country" inspired him and he recognized the possibility of educating an officer-class in Mexico that would be honorable, technically excellent, and socially adept.

In France he was commissioned to study at the School of Application in the School of Firing, where he studied under then Colonel Fayolle who excelled on the battlefield in World War I.

Ángeles was still abroad in late 1910 when he heard rumors of a revolt against President Porfirio Diaz. A soldier, even an academic, must be concerned by rumors of a revolt in his home country and on November 24 he requested a return to Mexico to fight against rebels led by Francisco I. Madero. Patriotism and sense of duty compelled his request, but he may have had additional motives. All his experience to date was academic: teaching or being taught. He wanted to be part of the action to test his theories in real-time. He was also ambitious. He knew officers are promoted more rapidly from the battlefield. However, on December 13, 1910 General Cosio responded to his request by a telegram saying the country was tranquil and his services were not needed at home.

Ironically, a few months later in May of 1911 Francisco I. Madero defeated the federal army of President Porfirio Diaz and it was Diaz who went into exile. Actually, Diaz resigned and went to live in Europe.

How could a mild-mannered man like Madero defeat the Federal Army? Corruption and deceit within that army combined to make it a paper army, just as Ángeles had warned. The number of troops was exaggerated by the generals in order to line their own pockets with pesos intended for non-existent troops; the same was true of arms and ammunition. What remained was a sham army of poorly trained and poorly armed conscripts that collapsed before the determination of Madero.

Before Ángeles left France, he was awarded the Medal of the Legion of Honor for contributions made to France. The medal is the highest honor of merit bestowed by the French Republic, without regard to birth or religion, nationality or sex. The medal was created by Napoleon Bonaparte on May 29,1792 to honor those who uphold liberty and equality. It was not given lightly. Colonel Felípe Ángeles received the award because he, with others, redesigned the hydraulic brakes of the Schneider-Cannet canon, France's standard artillery piece in the 1800s. His textbooks on the theory of firing were used at military schools in Belgium and France.

Ángeles was fortunate to be abroad during military actions against strikers at mines in Caananea and wars against the Yaquis in Sonora. And being in France kept him far away from political in-fighting of army cliques at home. Meanwhile, his international recognition added status to the Military College of Chapultepec.

CHAPTER TWO

The Military School at Chapultepec

F rancisco I. Madero began his presidency with the long-term goal of educating Mexicans in principles of democracy while weaning them away from strong-man rule. He taught democracy by his example of respecting all existing institutions including the military. He dissolved the revolutionary fighters and expected the federal army to perform their duties. He planned to change the army gradually from the inside by building a new officers corp. Therefore, the choice of director of the Military College was crucial to his goal.

Choosing Colonel Felípe Ángeles to direct the creation of a professional military was not difficult. Ángeles was the obvious choice for several reasons. For years his classmates had jokingly called him the assistant director. They all knew his passion for the school. Internationally he was known for his textbooks and his work in France. His reputation for honesty was known and respected in both military and civilian circles. And even more fortunate, because of years abroad Ángeles was not part of any cliques existing within the old guard of the Porfirian regime.

Madero knew that in 1910 Ángeles requested a return to Mexico to protect the old dictator from Madero himself but that did not dissuade him. He made Ángeles director of the Military School at Chapultepec.

There is no record of Ángeles reaction when he received news of his appointment. Duty was always his first response to any command, but the irony of serving his previous enemy cannot have been lost on him. Yet this was an opportunity beyond any he had ever dreamed. To be able to effect change in an institution he loved and receive a general's star as well was doubly exhilarating. He left France the last days of December 1911 and arrived at the port of Vera Cruz in January of 1912.

Reorganizing the Military School

Felípe Ángeles became Director of the Military School of Mexico at Chapultepec on January 8, 1912. His first priority was to build a professional officer class by establishing traits missing in years past. A lack of honor and pride in excellence had corrupted and weakened the army of Diaz and diminished the reputation of the school. This was a position he was uniquely qualified to fill. The military school had been his home since the age of fourteen. Like no other he knew the traditions, the honors, and strengths of the school, as well as its weaknesses. He relished the opportunity ahead.

His years in France enlarged his thinking; the French military was the world's most respected at that time. At St. Cyr he learned what a military school could be. His goal was to prepare officers who would excel in all circumstances, from directing troops on a battlefield to carrying on an interesting conversation at a dinner party. He knew officers would need a broad general knowledge of literature, languages, history, and geography as well as mathematics and science. He even insisted on dancing lessons. His curriculum faced ridicule and scorn from well-established cliques within the old guard. But he was backed by the president and cadets enthusiastically embraced the new curriculum.

President Madero sought to encourage Felípe Ángeles by inviting him to ride with him through Chapultepec Park. Both were excellent horsemen, and they enjoyed one another's company. A close friendship developed. Ángeles admired the president. He later wrote, "Madero was a brave citizen, rising up from the bedrock of a public accustomed to respect the will of the dictator...'.[8] Those words could have described Ángeles himself, for in his entire lifetime he had never questioned the dictatorship of President Diaz.

On long rides together they discussed plans to create a world-renowned military school and a democratic nation. Of the nation Madero said, "I will lead them to democracy in spite of themselves," referring to the institutions of Mexico.[9] To critics who thought he should act quickly and forcefully, he answered, it would be hypocritical to resort to dictatorial methods to lead the country to democracy. He would show them by example and expect each institution to do its job. Many were surprised to see Madero immediately disband his revolutionary army and rely solely on the existing federal army which for thirty years had been loyal to President Diaz. The group that made these feelings known was called Renovators. They supported the revolution but questioned Madero's methods. Naïve and weak were terms his critics used to describe him.

Madero's vision was a nation in which all classes of society had a voice. Madero recognized that with an effective vote citizens could change the nation peacefully. There would be no need for bloodshed or dangerous confrontation. But that required time and patience.

Ángeles was attempting to effect change in the military in much the same patient manner. He planned to change the military from the inside by preparing honorable officers to overcome an existing culture of corruption.

The immediate problem for Mexico was a treasury swept clean by Diaz when he left office. Solutions to many problems hinged on finances. For example, Madero had promised land reform to the peasants, but to be able distribute land required ability to pay for it. Madero would not expropriate land from the present owners. To buy and legally distribute land to Zapata's peasants could not be accomplished until the government had money. Madero was satisfied that the results of the election were powerful enough to accomplish all the changes he had promised. He had made limited progress toward achieving the aims of the revolution, but he needed time. The financial need was in the process of being solved by a low-interest loan for $100,000,000 from France. The loan was arranged by the interim president, but not yet in hand. The fulfillment of Madero's promise to the farmers of Morelos was delayed.

War of resistance

Meanwhile, the cost of fighting other problems was significant. His new government was faced with a well-organized war of resistance from many sources.. When Madero was swept into office in November 1911 by a popular wave of the disenfranchised, opposition to his presidency ran deep. Those who loved the power and special considerations they received under Porfirio Diaz did not propose to allow 'that dreamer' to upset the system. This secret war began before Madero was sworn in as president. The old guard of the army sought to weaken all pro-Madero generals gradually by allowing their requests for men and provisions to go unfilled. Foreign business groups such as railroads, oil companies, sugar producers, and mine owners, joined generals made wealthy by corruption and composed a group of influential people who wanted a return to the days of Porfirio Diaz. They did not resign themselves to the new system but resisted, passively at first.

Madero expected a smooth transition of governmental power. Therefore, he left the incumbent bureaucratic framework in place. Methods of governance used by those holdover bureaucrats were harsh and exacerbated the suffering of the people, especially in the state of Morelos. Peasant farmers had no time to wait for their votes to bring changes. They expected immediate access to their land. Madero did not recognize the need for action was urgent.

In Madero's political manifesto, he promised land reform. Because of that the peasants in Morelos supported his presidency, but when those hopes were not fulfilled immediately they felt betrayed. Leaders in Morelos called meetings to address their problem and presented Madero with their summary, the *Plan de Ayala*, a declaration of war that states: 'because the inept president[10] Madero has broken his promises, we the people of Morelos withdraw our support'.

The elders of the state of Morelos anointed Emilio Zapata to represent them because Emilio had once worked in Mexico City as a stable hand and could speak Spanish. Zapata accepted their trust solemnly and his focus never wavered. Later following the murder of Madero, Villa and Carranza encouraged him to help destroy their mutual enemy the assassin Huerta, but he continued to do only that which would help the peasants of Morelos. What followed was not a formal war but guerilla attacks against large land holders. Haciendas were raided, crops burned, and bridges destroyed.

An undeclared war was carried out by the press. Newly freed from absolute censorship, instead of factually reporting the accomplishments of the new government, they turned to sensationalism. Wild stories of atrocities by Zapata and every bit of gossip and rumor, and even concocted slanderous lies were printed against Madero and his family.

The Rebellion of Bernardo Reyes

Adding to Madero's difficulties were uprisings in other parts of Mexico. On December 13, 1911 General Bernardo Reyes called for rebellion against the Madero government. Reyes was a high ranking retired general friend and supporter of Porfirio Diaz. Moreover, he considered himself the obvious successor to Diaz. Reyes wanted to reenact Madero's triumphal march from the border to the capitol with himself dramatically leading from horseback. He was certain he could count on thousands of armed men to answer to his call and meet him at Mexico's northern the border. But he overestimated his popularity and prestige and by December 25 he surrendered to the surprised rural barracks commander in Linares (Nuevo Laredo). From there he telegraphed General Trevino, Chief of the Third Zone and reported: "I called the army and the people, but not a single man came to my support…I place myself at your disposition." [11]

Reyes was arrested and sent to Mexico City where he was found guilty of the crime of rebellion and held in the Prison of Santiago Tlaltelolco in Mexico City.

The Rebellion of Felix Diaz

Revolt begets revolt and soon Felix Diaz, nephew of the exiled dictator, made a bungled attempt to lead a revolt in the state of Vera Cruz. It was quickly put down by local authorities who Felix Diaz mistakenly thought would come over to his side. Felix was convicted of treason, a crime punishable by death, but like General Reyes, Felix Diaz was not executed. Rather, he was jailed in Lecumberri prison in Mexico City. From prison he remained in close contact with General Reyes and General Manuel Mondragon and together continued to plot the destruction of President Madero.

The Rebellion of Pasqual Orozco

In January of 1912 Orozco was persuaded by Madero to serve as chief of the Rurales in the state of Sinaloa. That was an effort to make use of his irregular military experience as well as to purchase his loyalty. However, Orozco felt he had been 'repaid with ingratitude'. After two months he quit that job, gathered the remains of his revolutionary army and moved against the Madero government.

Orozco, a tall, rangy second-generation Basque, has been described as a mule skinner, but his mule trains were actually a successful transportation business. On narrow mountain trails, too rugged for trucks, he delivered ore from the silver mines to smelters. Mules were the only possible means of transportation. Orozco was a well-respected entrepreneur.

The responsibility to quell the revolt of Orozco fell to loyal General Garcia Salas, one of the generals being systematically stripped of men and supplies by the federal army. Consequently, Garcia Salas failed to stop Orozco. The Battle of Rellenos was particularly humiliating to him and following a crushing defeat he retired to his railroad car, wrote a farewell note and shot himself.

The death of that honorable man was a tragedy for the nation, and for the Madero regime. Because Reyes and Diaz were in prison, Madero lacked generals to handle the Orozco revolt. In order to put down Orozco in Chihuahua, Madero began to play musical chairs with his generals, he transferred General Victoriano Huerta from the war zone in Morelos to the one in Chihuahua.

Francisco (Pancho) Villa brought men to fight with Huerta against Orozco because of his respect for Madero. Villa, who was Orozco's comrade-in-arms at the battle of Juarez, was incensed by Orozco's treachery. Loyalty was the core of Villa's character and Villa loved the president. He described Madero as "a little man with a big heart." He despised Orozco and all his men, who were known as red flaggers. Villa gave them no mercy in battle. He took no prisoners. When reprimanded about the rules of war, Villa responded, "I didn't know war was a game".

Villa did not think of himself or his men as part of the federal army. He fought Orozco in his own way. Victoriano Huerta did not like Villa. Huerta was regular army and he felt contempt for all irregulars, and Villa in particular. Villa was an effective leader but difficult to control. Conflict was inevitable. An opportunity to get rid of him came when Villa's men seized a fine mare as booty and a complaint was made. Huerta ordered Villa to return the mare. Villa refused. Without benefit of court martial to which Villa was entitled, Huerta ordered him shot for insubordination. The sergeant of the firing squad scratched an X on the wall with his bayonet and ordered

Villa to stand in front of it. Villa emptied his pockets, gave his watch and his money to those who were about to shoot him, and prepared to die. Alerted, Raul Madero, rushed to telegraph his brother, the president. Rifles were raised, "Ready, Aim…"… the squad was ready to fire. The telegram arrived sparing Villa's life and ordering him sent to Mexico City for trial. He was jailed in Tlalteleloco prison. It was there that Villa first learned to read[12].

General Huerta succeeded against Orozco where Garcia Salas had failed. But Chihuahua remained a troubled and divided state under his military rule. Meanwhile, violence increased in the state of Morelos because General Aurelio Blanquet was left in charge to continue the genocidal tactics of Huerta against the Zapatistas.

Madero confided fully in Ángeles. When the president would leave the capitol city on working tours, the soldier accompanied him. On his part Madero was assured and enthusiastic about the changes that Ángeles was bringing to the Military College. The growing friendship was no secret and many in the military were jealous.

In August when the war with Zapata and the pressures of the presidency seemed impossible President Madero turned to General Ángeles whom he knew was the only general who understood his goals and was capable of convincing Zapata that his promises to the Zapatistas would be fulfilled… in time.

CHAPTER THREE

Reassignment to Cuernavaca

It was mid-August when Felípe Ángeles received orders to go to Cuernavaca and become the Military Governor of the 7th Military District of Mexico. This was an abrupt change for General Ángeles; his entire career had been academic either as a student or a teacher. Now he was ordered to govern a war zone. Changes he had made in the curriculum of the school were beginning to bear fruit; he was with his family and supremely content. He must have regretted leaving the Military School at Chapultepec.

However, without question he packed his bags, chose his staff, and took the next train to Cuernavaca. His new headquarters would be in Cuernavaca, the capital city of the State of Morelos. Ángeles understood why President Madero found it critical to send him to Morelos. The peace of the nation was being threatened by Zapata and his guerilla attacks against bridges, roads and the enormous haciendas. The Indian population that Madero desired to empower was being persecuted by an uncooperative federal army. Consequently, Madero's administration was in crisis, and he was losing popular support. Who else could Madero rely on to work with Zapata, not torment him? It is quite likely both men considered this change a temporary one.

Ángeles chose five officers from the college to be his aides. Among them were Captain Gustavo Barzan and Captain Jose Gonzales Heron, (Gonzalitos).

Surprisingly, Captain Federico Cervantes, Ángeles most ardent disciple, was not one of the five. A few months earlier, when Orozco revolted in Chihuahua, Cervantes requested to go north and fight him. President Madero asked Ángeles' opinion of the move and Ángeles made a better suggestion. He thought that Cervantes would be a good candidate to send to France to study aeronautics and prepare to build Mexico's first air force.

Governing a military district was a new responsibility for Ángeles for which he had no time to prepare. He wrote to his friend Manuel Marquez Sterling, the Cuban ambassador to Mexico: "I was concerned at having been sent to direct the War of the South in the vast territory of five states, Morelos, Pueblo, Mexico, Tlaxcala and Guerrero without having been allowed a few days to go to the state where the campaign was being fought."[13]

On the 12th of August 1912, Ángeles and his staff took the train to Cuernavaca, which would be Ángeles headquarters for the foreseeable future. That city was the colonial capital of conquistador Hernan Cortez, and is the present-day capital of the state of Morelos.

As the train entered the sullen domain of Emiliano Zapata, Ángeles tried to envision the monumental task that lay ahead and where pitfalls might lie.[14] He knew he had much to learn.

From the window of the train Ángeles observed troops in formation awaiting him at the entrance of the city of Cuernavaca. He wrote, "They were perishing without food, their faces yellow, their uniforms filthy. "Where are their quarters, I asked? Poor soldiers, they live in an inclement climate at a high altitude, where the rains rarely stop, and they don't have even a patch of dry ground where they can stretch out to sleep?"[15]

Before Ángeles arrival, commander followed commander in rapid succession, but none was able to put down Zapata and his untrained followers.[16] The Zapatistas were not an army; they were a people in arms protecting their homes. Men became fighting demons because they and their families were persecuted. They were completely dedicated to their cause. Federal troops, in contrast, were conscripts, poorly paid and ill-treated.

Two nights before Ángeles arrived in Morelos there was a massacre of twenty soldiers. It occurred on the road between Cuernavaca and Mexico City. Those who committed the massacre were known to be from Zapata's peasant Army of the South, a group led by Zapata's best general, Genovevo de la O. This was Ángeles introduction to the name of the legendary warrior. Genovevo de la O was a name the general would come to respect.

A detachment of soldiers managed to capture a spy, but poorly trained as they were, they did not set guards and the spy escaped. The following night while the soldiers slept the unguarded camp was set upon by Genovevo's men and wiped out. Emotions were high in Cuernavaca when Ángeles arrived. The troops wanted revenge and any Indian was thought to be a deserving target.

The goal of General Ángeles was to change the situation in Morelos by diplomatic means not genocide. Officers trained by Juvencio Robles, Ángeles' immediate predecessor, agreed with his ruthless policy. They resisted Ángeles' new policies. While they did not mutiny outright, they grumbled and delayed. Ángeles believed they were good men who were 'saturated with anti-indigenous prejudice.'[17] Knowing that opinions are not changed by words, he began to modify the attitudes of his officers through first-hand experiences. Simultaneously, he went about changing the pathetic conditions of the mistreated soldiers by insisting on adequate provisions, and personal cleanliness.

To begin his campaign of diplomacy aimed at the general population of Morelos, he chose a village that had been ravaged by federal troops. The houses had been burned and the citizens were living in the forests, homeless and starving.

He waited for a day when he knew no bodyguard would be available, then ordered a few of his officers to accompany him to a village that had been ravaged. The officers explained to him that they could not go until there were troops available to accompany them. But Ángeles replied that they would pick up a few local guides as they passed through the next village. They could be armed he said. The group proceeded to the burned-out village. He spoke to the village leaders and encouraged them to begin anew. He began to rebuild the houses and sent soldiers to make the village habitable. Results were a slow but grudging change of opinion among his officers and a wary watchfulness from the villagers. Later he mentioned to a friend that his own mother was an Indian not unlike these villagers who were living exposed in the forests.[18]

He was criticized by many for not annihilating the Zapatista movement. His critics felt confused because he had the reputation of being a strong commander who was internationally recognized for artillery expertise and as the inventor of a powerful canon. They did not recognize that his limited military action demonstrated a deeper understanding of President Madero's goals.

One day a civilian official came to Ángeles' office warning that some of Genovevo's men had come to kill Ángeles. When asked how he knew, the man replied with a long convoluted and confusing story. Ángeles cut him short and told him to have the men brought to his office. When they arrived a week later he was surprised to see they were the same men whose houses he had ordered rebuilt. When told of the charge they asked the name of their accuser. Ángeles told them and they responded, "That explains it. That man has made us much trouble. He was a spy for General Robles. Because of him many in our village were killed." Ángeles believed them and sent them away. A few days later another civilian official called to say he was holding prisoner some men who had attacked him. Again, they turned out to be the same men who had 'tried to assassinate' him. "Where are their guns?" I asked.

"We couldn't find them," was the reply. Ángeles told the official that he believed them blameless and ordered their release. The official was incredulous.[19]

Ángeles could see that the official had attempted to involve him in local affairs, but he didn't understand why. When Ángeles told this story to his friend and confidant, Patricio Leyva, governor of Morelos, Leyva explained that the root of the matter was a disagreement between the town of Santa Maria and the hacienda of Temixco. The dispute was over a huge piece of land which ex-president Diaz had given to the former mayor, Manuel Alacron. Delegates from Santa Maria had been appointed, then bribed, to rule for the owners of the hacienda, who paid only $15,000 pesos for the purchase. (In 1912 peso and dollar were par). The new owners found it easy to describe the previous owners as untamed rebels who should be exterminated. The whole plot was made legal by the shameful Lerdo Law,[20] which ruled until Madero was elected. At that time the town revived corrective litigation. This intrigue was empowered by a threat from General Juvencio Robles, the commander Ángeles replaced: Robles promised, "If the town won't submit, my troops will take care of it". And so there followed the Battle of Santa Maria, portrayed by the press in Mexico City as a glorious victory. Almost all officers involved were promoted.

Disturbed by such deception Ángeles asked, "What in truth had happened? The inhabitants, with only a few weapons, battled heroically and it was some time before they were defeated. Troops entered and killed many innocents. Among the dead was the family of Genoveva de la O, who then took up arms and was transformed from a charcoal maker into an enemy of injustice."

Resistance within the high command of the Federal army was an active conspiracy; a secret war to destroy Madero. Sabotage began before Madero took office and never ceased. Their plotting cost the life of General Garcia Salas who was defeated when his army of 600 men was sent to fight against Orozco who led 6,000 men. The same tactics were used to weaken Ángeles. "Without saying a word, they are removing my troops," he wrote to President Madero. "The 52 men they have just removed from Medina Barron on the Chalco line were intended to be taken from Guerrero of Vicario. I have maintained the situation by means of moving detachments from place to place, much to the displeasure of the inhabitants of villages and haciendas, and the troops who have suffered undue fatigue. It is dangerous to continue in this way."[21]

Ángeles knew that Zapata and Madero were natural allies. They held the same goals: "liberty, justice and decent living conditions for the masses". Madero knew that the citizens of Morelos were now free to control their conditions by electing their own leaders. It saddened him to see the tragedy of one-time fellow revolutionaries turning on one another[22]," Ángeles wrote to the Cuban ambassador. "I would give anything to show these people the mistake they are making. President Madero is doing the best he can for them, but he needs cooperation."[23]

President Madero was well-intentioned. However, he was badly served by those from the Diaz administration held over in their positions who sabotaged his goals "[24]

One weapon used in their undeclared war was the legal system. Pablo Escandon, well respected owner of several large haciendas was arrested at his hacienda, El Jabali in San Luis Potosi. Authorities in San Luis Potosi had intercepted a message from Escandon to Zapata that contained funds for horses and supplies. It was money extorted by the Zapatistas to not burn or destroy Escandon's haciendas. Zapata called this a 'revolutionary tax'. With this evidence the judge sentenced Escandon to prison.

Escandon was formally declared a prisoner and entered the Lecumbari prison in Mexico City at 11:30 on the morning of November 13th, 1912. He was assigned a special cell designated for political prisoners and there he passed the night.[25] Conditions in the prison were grim. Cells were uncomfortable and it was extremely cold. On the morning of November 14, Ernesto Madero, (brother of the president) who was a cabinet member, appeared before the judge and declared that he would be responsible for the innocence of Escandon. He also mentioned that if they suspended the cane harvest because of threats by the rebels, "all workers put out of work will join the Zapatistas". The administrator of the hacienda received permission to deliver the extortion money to the Zapatista chief, Amador Salazar.[26]

Released from prison, Escandon was met by his family and friends at the prison gates. But before he was driven away, he asked the jailor how many prisoners remained in prison. Three hundred he was told. Escandon delivered three hundred blankets to the prison that afternoon to ease the misery of prisoners who would endure another night.

The anti-Madero press assisted the conspirators by reporting that almost all the hacendados made similar contributions to Zapata and were justified in doing so to protect their properties and save the agricultural riches of the nation. The purpose of this emotionally charged incident was to demonstrate that the Madero government was unable to protect landowners. Ángeles recognized the imprisonment of Escondon for the political ploy it was: hostile propaganda aimed at turning hacienda owners against Madero

The Battle of La Trinchera

The five captains on Ángeles staff were from as many parts of Mexico. Captain Gonzalitos happened to have grown up in the nearby area of La Trinchera. One day Gonzalitos went on foot from Cuernavaca towards Mexico (the state not the city) to visit his home village. His route went past the mountain La Trinchera. Later that morning Ángeles heard that Zapatistas had killed a newspaper boy on the road at the foot of the mountain La Trinchera. He also believed for a short while that Gonzalitos was killed as well, although he soon learned by telephone that Gonzalitos ducked into the bush and continued by another path.

The next day Ángeles learned that Zapatistas detained and robbed some soldiers at the same spot near La Trinchera. He ordered a detachment from Cruz de Piedra, the nearest military unit, to throw the enemy off the mount. The forces of that detachment battled the enemy and reported to Ángeles that the enemy was destroyed. Ángeles later learned that this report was false. The detachment had been shot at by the enemy and retired to Cruz de Piedra. The captain in charge, Captain Osorno, reported this to Colonel Viruegas at Cruz de Piedra. Ángeles informed Colonel Viruegas in Cruz de Piedra that the Zapatistas were still in place and they were numerous.

Ángeles resisted believing that an officer as brave and chivalrous as Osorno could give a false report, so he went to verify Viruegas' report. Another reason for his expedition was the fact that Gonzalitos would return on foot along the same route that afternoon. Therefore, after eating lunch he decided to personally reconnoiter with only his staff officers. On the road, however, he had second thoughts. If by chance they were attacked by the Zapatistas and one of his officers killed, the press in the city would receive the news joyfully and broadcast his foolishness. He decided to obtain an escort from the detachment at Buena Vista, the hacienda nearest Cuernavaca. But the troops of that detachment were away on other service and only 13 foot-soldiers were available. That actually made his party more vulnerable because being on horseback without foot-soldiers they could easily escape the enemy if expedient, but with a small group of foot-soldiers to protect they could not escape. As it happened, Ángeles added 40 foot-soldiers he found in Cruz de Piedra and proceeded with a total of fifty three.

It was a coincidence that saved them from being destroyed. Ángeles stopped his soldiers and moved them off road to a wooded area for a training exercise in a place. They were not in view of the enemy. Zapatistas had seen them coming and were waiting in ambush, ready to open fire. If Ángeles had proceeded a little further, Zapatistas would have killed almost all of them in a few seconds and the few who were left would have dispersed.

The place where they stopped for training was about 200 meters from the site of the ambush where at least 500 men waited for Ángeles' patrol. As part of the exercise, Ángeles posted soldiers at the edge of the road and sent 15 of them, commanded by a sergeant, to serve as scouts. Their mission was to march toward La Trinchera and ascertain whether the hill had been abandoned. They were protected by the others who were stationed beside the road. When they advanced a few steps, the troops were exposed to the sight of the Zapatistas and were greeted by heavy fire that let them know not only the enemy's position, but also how numerous they were. It was impossible to reach La Trinchera for Ángeles men was stopped by a steep ravine. "We could not go forward, but neither could the enemy pursue us across that obstacle without danger… while there was daylight". Ángeles feared Zapatistas would encircle them and cut off their retreat when it grew dark.

Gunfire alerted Gonzalitos to the situation as he returned toward Cuernavaca. He picked up an escort of 12 men from Huitzilac and they approached the battle along a path he knew well. Ángeles posted Gonzalitos' escort at the exit of a *vereda* (dry wash) and when the Zapatists advanced along the path Ángeles and his men were able to retreat. Ángeles plan was to rescue Gonzalitos, but it was Gonzalitos and his knowledge of the territory who saved Ángeles and his rescue team.

In days that followed, it was rumored that Zapatistas led by Genovevo were in the area between Mexico and Morelos, Ángeles with troops from the state of Morelos went on a joint maneuver with Major Riveroll's troops from the state of Mexico. The plan was to approach quietly from two directions and trap Genovevo between them. However, Riveroll delayed for a week and then approached, making excessive noise. Ángeles circled through the village of Chalma and arrived after Riveroll. He found that Riveroll had contrived an excuse for a battle against the town. An old villager had pulled a rusty pistol in an attempt to protect his home. Riveroll hung him and a few others. An appalling scene met Ángeles when he arrived a few minutes later. He questioned the villagers and listened to their grim descriptions. It was an unnecessary carnage against relatively unarmed villagers. Ángeles wrote, "It happened so near to me, almost in my presence." [27]

He sent Riveroll back to his base in the state of Mexico and took his own troops back to Cuernavaca. His return took him along a high ridge from which he could look down upon the beautiful valley of Toluca and see Riveroll and his troops moving below. As he watched he was sickened to see them burning crops on either side of their route. He soon learned that Genovevo was watching the same destruction from another hilltop.

Questions troubled Ángeles. He wrote, "Has society the right to protect despots who abuse the disinherited? Has society the right to permit assassinations of victims of vile intrigues by military chiefs? Must society tolerate the exploitation of a war that gives promotions to officers at the cost of lives and families? Can society look away from the horrors of burned cities, churches turned to stables, and Indians turned from their towns?"[28]

"The presence of General Ángeles as the new commander marked a peaceful interlude when something of the old civility returned briefly to Cuernavaca," wrote Rosa King, owner of the Bella Vista Hotel where Ángeles lived. "I felt in him a quality that I missed in his predecessors, a quality of mercy and a willingness to understand."[29] By the time Ángeles left Cuernavaca his troops were the best trained in the entire federal army.

There were no more Zapatista raids into the city and villagers who had been active defenders began to return to their crops and families. Zapata continued to attack railroads and haciendas but attacks became sporadic and less violent. By December the situation had calmed enough for Ángeles to feel it safe to bring his family to Cuernavaca for the holidays. He told Clarita to come and bring their nine-year old twins, Julio and Felípe. The grounds of the Hotel Bella Vista and the nearby Borda Gardens would be great places for them to explore. The two older children, Alberto and Isabel, may have been at boarding school.

In a spirit of great excitement Clara Krause de Ángeles, planned a joyful Christmas with her husband. She brought her sister to help with the boys. Clara and her sister Carmen were American born of Mexican-German descent. Carmen was blond and quiet like her

German father, but Clara was dark-haired and vivacious like her mother. The girls grew up in California and in 1897 Clara accepted a job teaching English at the American School in Mexico City. It was there that she met and married Felípe Ángeles.

The family's short trip to Cuernavaca began happily, but as they neared the city a band of Zapatistas swept out of the forest and attacked the train. The train stopped and Clara, realizing what was happening, gathered the boys and Carmen and quickly got off the train on the side away from the attackers and ran into the brush where they hid. When they could do so without being observed they moved toward Cuernavaca.

When news of the attack reached General Ángeles, he raced from his office, and with a small escort rushed to the stopped train. Zapatistas evaporated before them like a morning mist, and he found Clara safe and smiling; she was still picking twigs and thorns from her hair and clothing, but joyful to see her husband.

Señora Ángeles and the boys stayed in Cuernavaca the entire month of December. They lived at the Hotel Bella Vista, where Clara became lasting friends with Rosa King, the British widow who owned the hotel. Clara would begin each day asking, "Oh, Mrs. King what can we do today?" She wanted to be gay and unworried despite the unrest around her. They often took tea at the lovely Borda Gardens, or went on horseback rides and have picnics in the environs, never venturing too far from the city lest they fall into the hands of Zapatistas. Rosa King said, "Her presence made a great change in General Ángeles." His usual serious and thoughtful expression lightened.[30]

One afternoon the two women were sitting quietly in a shady corner of the patio watching hummingbirds dart among the roses, listening the water falling from a fountain, and laughing at the antics of the little boys. When the boy's *aya* (nurse) broke up the hilarity and took the boys away for a walk, Clara smiled and said almost to herself, "Oh, I do love my children and my family—but not like Felípe." Turning to Mrs. King she said, "If I seem to you a giddy woman, Senora King, it is because always I am afraid for him, if anything should happen to Felípe, I think I could not live." Without moving her quiet body, she suddenly turned her head half around so that her cheek lay against the braided chair back, and looking at me searchingly out of enormous eyes she asked, "Do you think, *amiguita*, that if something happened to Felípe, God would make me go on living without him?" Rosa King went on to say, "her question was often in my mind—and I had a premonition that I would live to see it answered."[31]

Christmas approached and the two women determined to have 'one last burst of gayety' to make life pleasant for the men who went out to fight, some to die, to keep them safe. They planned a *posada,* a Christmas party, and held it in the largest place Cuernavaca had to offer, the theatre. Each day was filled with excitement and mysterious preparations. Clara and Vera, Rosa King's daughter even made a trip to Mexico City to purchase decorations and inexpensive prizes. The theatre was lit with Japanese lanterns and brightly colored umbrellas with lights behind them.[32]

As each girl entered the door, she was given a fan with which to flirt. Four waiters from the hotel in black jackets and white gloves served the guests, and the military band, instead of martial music, played slow *danzas* as well as fox trots, a dance popular in that era. All fears and thoughts of war were pushed aside for one happy night and the whole town rejoiced.

When Senora Ángeles left Cuernavaca, anxiety returned and news from the capital became increasingly troubled. However, for Felípe January of 1913 began on a high note. He was called to Mexico City to be honored with a ceremony of appreciation and recognition for his services to the nation. A similar ceremony was held in Cuernavaca on February 5th. These were proud moments in his steadily rising career.

Four days later on the morning of February 9th all that changed.

CHAPTER FOUR

The Barracks Revolt

Gunfire awakened Mexico City before dawn. No one was surprised. For months rumors of a coup had swirled about the city, street to cobble-stoned street. The question was not if a coup would occur, but when. The conspirators were a clique of resentful generals who were bitter over the prospective loss of privileges that were threatened by President Madero and his new government.[1] Doubtless, the conspirators considered themselves patriots. Their goal was to rid the country of 'that dreamer' Francisco I. Madero, and bring back the comfortably corrupt ways of eighty-year-old Porfirio Diaz.

According to the conspirators' plan, Felix Diaz, nephew of Porfirio Diaz, would be the next strongman of Mexico, General Bernardo Reyes would be the transitional president and hold office until Felix Diaz was elected. That last objective was debatable in the mind of General Reyes because he considered himself the most able and therefore the most logical choice to replace Madero. But he did not press the matter.[33] Mondragon was to be the Minister of War, Rodolfo Reyes, the Minister of Justice. All officers in the conspiracy would receive advancement in rank and pay, and as before being given opportunities to become wealthier through patronage.

The man who first acted on their plan was retired General Manuel Mondragon. His calculating eyes and long wolfish features gave him the look of a villain and his name, Mondragon, 'my dragon' in French, has an ominous ring. He was retired, but he remained a powerful influence within the army of the previous regime.

However, that army was far from a cohesive entity in the winter of 1912. Those who had been made wealthy by serving the dictator Porfirio Diaz, controlled an army that was soft and corrupt. Its size and weaponry were exaggerated. Younger officers, colonels, captains and lieutenants were reluctant to participate in treason. General Mondragon mustered only 800 men and three batteries of artillery for his opening salvo in the coup. Of those forces 600 were cavalry cadets, young men from the military school at Tlalpan referred to as Aspirantes. These are not to be confused with cadets from the Military School at Chapultepec. None of them participated.

Saturday night, February 8th, preparing for the Sunday morning coup, Mondragon sent 400 cadets from the school of *Aspirantes in Tlalpan* to the National Palace. Those students conscripted streetcars in *Tacubaya*, rode to the *Zocolo* (central plaza), and were taken into the Palace by its treasonous commander, Col. Morales. Their orders were to be ready to throw open the gate for Generals Reyes and Felix Diaz when they arrived on Sunday morning.

What was intended to be a bloodless coup began to unravel when the main body was put off schedule by the extended morning ablutions of Felix Diaz. Another contributor to the unraveling was the failure to communicate that delay to the cadet group already in the Palace. The result was not fatal to the conspirators, but it delayed them long enough to turn a bloodless coup into a ten-day nightmare of bloody warfare in the central streets of Mexico City.

President Madero had been warned of a revolt many times. But in his effort to establish a democratic government, he naively ignored such rumors. He was determined to rely on the nation's existing institutions including the army, to be faithful to their duty to protect the nation and the elected government. He refused on principle to listen to rumors or warnings, so he ignored credible warnings came from family members and friends, among them, Felípe Ángeles.

Ángeles had firsthand information from Rafael Izquierdo, a colleague from his military school days, "You would be astonished at the names of those who are involved in the coup," Izquierdo said. Because of where Izquierdo was stationed Ángeles inferred that he was describing General Blanquet and Major Riveroll, officers from the state of Mexico. Ángeles most certainly warned Madero.

The governor of the state of Sonora, Jose Maria Maytorena warned Madero there were rumors of a coup plotted within Tlalalco prison which could ignite at any moment. Frustrated, Maytorena complained to Governor Abraham Gonzalez of Chihuahua it appeared that Madero did not consider the information of any importance.

Madero's own brother, Gustavo, warned him. Gustavo was alerted to the impending threat by an indebted friend who gave him names of eighteen conspirators. Convinced that the list was accurate, and because he was a man of action with great political savvy, he immediately formed a plan that he knew could work. Two of the eighteen men named, General Reyes and Felix Diaz, were already in prison charged with treason and he could see that other influential generals: Beltran, Navarette, and Blanquet, could be neutralized simply by transferring them to widely distant posts. General Mondragon and Rudolfo Reyes could be arrested or watched so closely that they would leave Mexico. The last name he saw on the list was General Victoriano Huerta. A question mark followed that name indicating that this man had not yet committed himself.[34] Gustavo recognized the urgency the situation, but putting any part of his plan into action required orders from the president.

With the names of conspirators in hand, Gustavo rushed to Madero and for an hour pleaded with him to act. But Madero, naïve, idealistic and stubborn, had an answer for every argument. His resistance disheartened Gustavo. "When he descended from the office of the president his face was flushed with the excitement of futile contention," wrote an American friend who awaited him. "Pancho (Madero) wouldn't believe it. He laughed at me," was all Gustavo would say.[35]

That disbelief would prove fatal.[36]

At Chapultepec Park

On the grounds of the military college in Chapultepec Park stood a grove of *ahuehuete* or cypress that was revered by the Aztecs of old because they believed there were two entrances to the underworld: one in Mitla, Oaxaca, and the other in a cave in Chapultepec park where the sacred entrance was hidden by trees. Aztec emperors protected the grove of trees and it continued to be protected by all governments after that. The protection was entrusted to Forest Guards who lived in small houses on the park grounds.[37]

In the wee hours of Sunday morning, one member of the Forest Guard heard the sounds of marching troops and clanking artillery. He looked out the window of his house toward the castle on the hill above but saw no lights or other signs of alarm. He wondered how President Madero or his staff, or the many cadets living at the Academy could not notice the ruckus caused by General Mondragon with 600 cadets with weapons and artillery. The guard correctly assumed that this was the rumored coup, but he did not report what he heard to superior officers because he was fearful that any interference would put him at cross-purposes with various cliques within the army. By chance, in those moments of indecision, one of few officers trusted by the Forest Guard, General Basso the Superintendent of the Palace, came walking home from the cities' late-night entertainments. The guard relayed his suspicions to

General Basso, thus relieving himself of further responsibility. Basso, who was equally aware of rumors of a coup, agreed with the guard. He did not inform the proper chain of command for similar reasons, but went instead a mile away to a house on *Avenida Londres* belonging to Gustavo Madero.[38]

Gustavo was still upset by the way his brother had dismissed his warning and consequently did not inform the president that the coup was underway. He knew this situation required immediate action; something the president was incapable of. It was not difficult for Gustavo to piece together exactly what was happening and even have a good estimate of a timetable for the conspirators to complete their plan.'[39] He decided the first actions of the traitors would be to go to Santiago Prison and release General Bernardo Reyes, then continue on to the Penitentiary to release Felix Diaz. Gustavo felt certain they would not actually reach the Palace before seven o'clock.[40] And he was certain that the commander within the palace would be ready to help them.

There was no time for Gustavo to summon aid. If the government were to be saved Gustavo would have to do it himself, or so he thought. Three men, Gustavo, Tomás his driver, and General Basso, set out immediately in Gustavo's touring car on an heroic if absurd mission to wrest the palace from hundreds of well-armed traitors.

What followed was a comic romp. According to Gustavo, he was allowed to enter the palace in his open car. Colonel Morales, the traitor in command of the Palace, immediately shouted, "You are under arrest"! Morales gave such a broad sweeping command to the cadets that 400 rifles were raised in unison, all pointing at Gustavo. The drama, or his bravado, brought Gustavo to his feet with a genuine roar of laughter. "Good morning, Colonel, what a fine host you are! I am rarely so warmly welcomed." Gustavo went on and on in a loud voice that all on the parade ground could hear. "It will be some time before the brave General Reyes and his friends arrive so let these young men stand at ease while we wait." The young men were snickering at the term 'brave' used to describe General Reyes for he had a reputation as one who led from behind. When Gustavo informed the men that they were also waiting for Felix Diaz who would need his beauty sleep and still must wax his mustaches, he had their attention, for Felix Diaz was known in the streets as '*el señorito*' for his foppish ways, The command began to shift from Colonel Morales to this outrageous civilian. The regular Palace Guard began to suspect that they were being involved in a coup along with the complicit cadets. Gustavo Madero claims that he managed to arrest Col. Morales and contain the coup.[41]

General Garcia Peña, Minister of War, also heard the suspicious sounds of revolt and became alarmed. He also went to the Palace in the early morning hours. His report, while not as entertaining as Gustavo's, is quite different. He claims that when he arrived at the Palace, he was arrested and confined to await the coming rebels. He agrees that Gustavo did come to the palace but at that point their reports diverge. Garcia Peña says that when Gustavo arrived it was he who was arrested and restrained.[42]

By six a.m. General Lauro Villar, the loyal commander of the post arrived on duty and took command. He released Peña and Gustavo and sent men to the walls above the gate to prepare for the arrival of the main body of traitors. Gustavo, his duty done, wisely left the situation in Villar's capable hands and went jauntily on his way to *Calle Marseille*, to the home of a friend, Angel Casio, and joined him there for breakfast.[43]

Conspirators March to the National Palace

As predicted by Gustavo, the conspirators marched directly to *Tlalalco Prison* to release General Reyes. That disciplined military man was waiting, prepared to assume his role as savior of Mexico. He was carefully dressed in uniform and wearing the cape of a commander. When the prison director objected to his prisoner being released, Mondragon and the group locked him into a cell. Reyes mounted a horse provided for him and joined the march to the *Penitentiary* to release General Diaz. The unfortunate director of that prison also offered resistance but was shot in the back by his own aide. The prisoner, Felix Diaz, apparently had been misinformed of the hour or he had simply overslept for he was still shaving when the rebels arrived. This delayed the march somewhat but not fatally. General Mondragon and his men waited for Felix Diaz to complete his morning ablutions, but General Reyes and 600 men including more cadets moved on to the Palace a mile away. They expected the Palace to be in rebel hands when they arrived.

Unfortunately, the drama that Gustavo had deemed over was only beginning. During the next three hours farce became tragedy. As predicted, the first group of insurrectionists led by General Reyes arrived at 7:00 am. General Gregorio Ruiz went ahead of the group expecting the gates of the Palace to be thrown open for them.

However, he was met and arrested by General Villar. A few minutes later when General Reyes approached the gate Villar called out, "Halt and surrender!" Reyes shouted back, "Open up, Lauro", and continued his advance. Shots were fired and General Reyes fell dead a few yards from the gate, his body riddled 'sieve-like' by machine gun fire.[44]

In the exchange of bullets General Villar was also wounded.[45] His collarbone was broken, a serious but not necessarily a fatal wound. However, Villar delayed treatment. He elected to remain on duty and go to the military hospital with his men. He died as a consequence.

Soldiers on the walls who were untrained and unfamiliar with the destructive power of machine guns continued spraying bullets across the Zocalo, killing hundreds of civilians.[46]

The second group of insurgents led by Felix Diaz, at last properly bathed and shaved approached the Palace on a street parallel to that used by General Reyes. When they heard gunfire and realized that the coup had gone terribly wrong they made an abrupt turn and marched double time to safety provided by thick walls of the *Ciudadela*. There, they set up their headquarters and were soon joined by surviving insurgents retreating from the confrontation at the National Palace.

President Madero Learns of the Revolt

At his residence, the Castle in *Chapultepec* Park, Madero awoke and learned about the events of the morning. He was one of the last to know. After he was informed he insisted that his place was at the Palace. The president, a fine horseman, mounted one of his favorite horses and galloped down Chapultepec hill with an escort of twenty cadets from the Military Academy. He then placed himself in front of mounted police that were already gathered there and as they marched down the length of the *Paseo de la Reforma*; assistants of the *Estado Mayor* came rushing out of their houses and joined them. Various members of the Cabinet dashed down the steps of their residences while still buttoning their jackets. Party members joined the ranks and from the lower classes came *peons* who loved the president faithfully. A taxi approached the parade of patriots and from the cab a man descended. He was dressed as a civilian and was wearing blue sunglasses. He was General Victoriano Huerta. He came over to the president, offered his services and joined the march to the Palace. On the *Avenida Juarez* members of the public applauded the president and his company. Nothing untoward occurred until they reached the *Bellas Artes* building (the National Theatre). Machine gun fire could be heard from the direction of the *Zocalo* and the Calle de Plateros.

In spite of wounds he received during his earlier arrest, General Garcia Peña met the advancing group on the *Paseo* and the president dismounted to discuss the matter with his Minister of War. Peña wisely advised caution and convinced the president to send out scouts. Huerta then intervened and advised the president to return to the Castle. Both men insisted that Madero must not expose his person. As if to confirm Huerta's position, the party heard more shots being fired and realized that bullets came from nearby and were aimed at Madero. Someone was firing from the nearby balcony of the *Palacio de Bellas Artes*; a man standing beside the president fell dead. Huerta spoke the truth; it was a dangerous place to be. The entire group, Ministers, guards, and police, all quickly entered into the Daguerre Photo Shop near them on the Paseo. The Minister of War warned that the situation was insecure, that there was imminent risk for Madero and asked for instructions. Huerta took advantage of the situation and proposed that he be allowed to put things in order. Two scouts then brought back a detailed account. "The Palace is in loyal hands," they said. Madero put an end to dithering by re-mounting his horse and turning its head toward the *Zocalo*. 'He looked like a conqueror and the crowd acclaimed him as such. It was nearly nine o' clock when he reached the huge plaza.[47] There he met a scene of indescribable carnage. Scattered across the square were several hundred bodies. Some were those of curious *peons* drawn by sounds of early morning gunfire. Their bodies now lay mingled among those of penitents who had come from early mass at the Cathedral, some still holding rosaries in lifeless hands. The body of General Bernardo Reyes lay in front of the Palace gate.

President Madero Takes Charge

Once inside the Palace, Madero found General Villar near death. That must have been an electrifying moment for him as he realized that every word spoken by Gustavo was true and his list of conspirators accurate. Though shaken by this revelation, Madero took charge of the situation. Many things demanded his immediate attention. He began by having the body of General Reyes brought into the Palace and then allowing Red Cross personnel to clear the wounded and dead from the Zocolo. He met informally with those cabinet members who had come to the Palace and together they ordered the execution of General Gregorio Ruiz and all those actively involved in treason. Col. Morales was killed earlier in the fighting. Madero listened to the regular Palace Guards as they pleaded ignorance and promised their loyalty. He believed them and forgave their unknowing part in the attempted coup. The cadets from the military school at *Tlalpan* however were proven traitors. They were not forgiven. Fifty-two cadets were executed for treason.

It was obvious that General Villar must be replaced immediately and Madero appointed the only available general of sufficient seniority, Victoriano Huerta. Villar with his last breaths pleaded with Madero not to appoint this man whom he knew to be a dishonest drunkard. However, feeling he had no choice, Madero made Huerta the Chief of all the armies of Mexico. There is no doubt his appointment was intended to be temporary until he could be replaced by Felípe Ángeles, but in the crisis it was not feasible to leave the position unfilled.[48]

General Huerta carried out the executions with more than his usual efficiency. Some suggest his conduct was motivated by a desire to prove his loyalty to Madero and to convince those who protested his appointment, while others suspect he wanted to silence men who knew that his sympathies were with the insurgents. He carried out the grim tasks within the confines of the National Palace. [49]

Madero sent telegrams to each of Mexico's state governors telling them of the attempt and assuring them that the situation was under control. With these measures attended to, he turned his thoughts to other problems. With new eyes he pondered what kind of protection he could expect from his military. It appeared that only a few discontented generals were involved in the conspiracy, but they were very influential men. Who else might they have influenced; in whom could he place his trust?

Cabinet member Manuel Bonilla says that the president left the Palace at about three o'clock on Sunday afternoon to go to the station to catch a train to Cuernavaca.[50] However, the president did not leave by train. For some reason he went by automobile, in an open touring car with his aides, Gustavo Garamendia and Federico Montes, Deputy Alejandro Ugarte, stenographer Elias de los Rios and Alfredo Alvarez. He wanted to confer with General Ángeles and their mutual friend Patricio Leyva the ex-governor of Cuernavaca. On this trip Madero's companions expressed concern about naming Huerta as Military Commander of the armed forces. Madero agreed the nomination was a regrettable compromise and that on his return he would replace Huerta with Felípe Ángeles.

Ángeles Prepares to Protect the President
On Sunday February 9, 1913, General Ángeles began his sixth month in command of the Military Zone in Morelos. He was still glowing from appreciation shown him by the president for his services to the nation and he was pleased with the progress he was making in controlling the army of Zapata. Although Zapata continued

his attacks on haciendas and railroads, promising negotiations were underway.

A phone call alerted Ángeles that a coup attempt was underway at the National Palace. The coup was expected, what was unexpected was the decision of the president to come Cuernavaca to speak to him. Why would the president make such a risky trip? Why not simply order Ángeles to the Palace in Mexico City, a much safer and simpler plan? He did not openly question the president instead prepared to protect him.

There were many dangers to confront. On one hand he foresaw a threat from a rebellious faction within the army and on the other, there was still a danger from Zapata and his peasant army which controlled much of the territory between Mexico City and Cuernavaca. Another possible threat was within the city of Cuernavaca itself. Zapata was the most respected man in the state of Morelos, far more popular than the president. Ángeles realized that even if the president could reach Cuernavaca safely he could yet be attacked by civilian mobs. Ángeles was already dangerously understaffed and undersupplied, now he was asked to protect the president, control the state of Morelos, and at the same time protect the town of Cuernavaca from Zapata's raids.

To meet the crisis, he assembled what assets he could to protect the president. Although his troops were few they had become the most disciplined of the federal army. He contacted Zapata and sent protection money. "Zapata was always short of money and he never went back on a promise".[51]

Because Ángeles knew that the president was traveling without escort, he sent a railroad repair train loaded with seventy-five soldiers as far as Tres Marias to provide an escort for the president for the last few miles into the city of Cuernavaca.

One additional preparation made by Ángeles for the visit by the president was to enlist the help of his British friend Rosa King the owner of the Bella Vista Hotel. Rosa King recalls:

> "Sunday afternoon, as I was coming down the staircase, I was met by a very smart-looking officer, a stranger to me, who addressed me in perfect

English... He told me that President Madero was coming to Cuernavaca for a night, and he wished to make arrangements for him and his party to stay at the Bella Vista."[52]

Usually when President and Mrs. Madero came to Cuernavaca, as they often did, they stayed at the home of their friend Mr. Carreon. When Mrs. King expressed her surprise, the officer said, "Mrs. King, the President must not stay in a private house, his life is in danger. While he is here, we ask that you take him under the protection of your roof and the British flag."

When Mrs. King told the officer that as a foreigner she should not be drawn into the politics of her host country, the officer replied, "Oh, Mrs. King, General Ángeles sent me to you and said he knew you would do all you could to help us." When she heard that General Ángeles had sent him, she realized the danger must be severe and she gave her frightened consent. Her first action was to raise the British flag in which she had 'unshakable trust'[53].

Ángeles met Madero and his companions at the station in Cuernavaca. The afternoon and early evening hours were spent with Patricio Leyva, the former governor of Morelos. Later they all dined together at the Bella Vista Hotel and discussed the situation for hours. Finally, it was decided that it would be best for Madero to remain in Cuernavaca while Felípe Ángeles took soldiers to Mexico City to take control of the crisis. The soldiers were started on their way and Ángeles planned to catch up with them later.[54]

As Mrs. King and President Madero sat in the lounge after dinner a mob gathered outside the hotel shouting, "Death to Madero". The president immediately sprang up saying, "Excuse me, Mrs. King, I must go and speak to them." She begged him not to go and sent for General Ángeles thinking he would have more influence than she did. Ángeles came at once and would not hear of Madero addressing the crowd. He went out to the balcony and the people soon quieted down. When he returned he told us that people had dispersed and were going back to their homes. "His manner was so quiet and easy, as though the matter had been of no consequence, and as though he had not risked his own life." Seeing the two men together it struck Mrs. King that "the love Ángeles had for Madero was much the protective feeling of a big boy for the little boy who was in for it."[55]

Monday February 10, 1913

By morning the plans of the previous night changed abruptly. President Madero decided his place was at the National Palace and so with Filipe Ángeles he returned to the capital. As they left the hotel the expression of concern on the face of Mrs. King caused the president to smile and say, "Why, Mrs. King I will be quite safe, I have my troops with me." She turned to General Ángeles and he said, "We go to join Huerta, the new Commander in Chief". The name Huerta came as an ominous shock to Mrs. King for both she and Ángeles knew the man's character, his drunkenness, his neglect and mistreatment of his own troops as well as his cruelty toward the peasants of Morelos during his command of the state. Even worse, they shared an awareness that Huerta harbored deep personal hatred of Madero, because the scrupulously honest Madero once sacked Huerta for misplacing $50,000 pesos. That was a great humiliation for Huerta who was merely following what had been standard procedure under the Diaz administration. "I am not a bookkeeper, I am a general," was Huerta's arrogant reply.[56] That humiliation was not forgotten and would be avenged.

CHAPTER FIVE

Ten Tragic Days

resident Madero and General Ángeles left Cuernavaca together and returned to Mexico City. Before entering the capital President Madero arranged for members of his cabinet to meet them at a place between Xochomilco and Tepepan. At this emergency meeting the president announced to his cabinet his decision to replace Huerta with Felípe Ángeles as Commander in Chief of the Armies. Alberto Garcia Peña, Secretary of War, immediately rejected that plan. The idea was unthinkable, he explained. There was already bitter jealousy against Ángeles. To them he was merely a colonel whose rank of brigadier had not yet been confirmed by Congress. To elevate him to a position of authority over generals with greater seniority would not be acceptable to powerful military cliques who might well refuse to serve. Military seniority must be observed even in this emergency. Faced with that opposition Madero backed down although he was certain Ángeles was the correct choice for the position. Thus, Huerta remained Commander in Chief of all the armies, but Ángeles was named Chief of Staff of the Ministry of War. From those headquarters Ángeles could monitor the activity of the chiefs who did not inspire complete confidence.

Huerta remained in charge of routing conspirators from the Ciudadela and restoring peace to the city. Ángeles knew, as they all did, that Huerta was a poor choice to lead the army to rid the city of rebels, however, ineptitude and dishonesty do not equate to treason. Ángeles bowed to the decision of his chief and immediately placed himself under the command of the treacherous Huerta. Another fatal decision.

An alternative account of the cabinet meeting near Xochomilco claims that Secretary of War, Garcia Peña not only objected to the

Pappointment of Ángeles as Commander in Chief, but actually disobeyed President Madero's verbal appointment making Ángeles Chief of Staff. Instead, General Garcia Pena went with Ángeles by automobile, not to headquarters of the General Staff, but to a military post at the corner of the Calle Colon and ordered him to stay there and not leave without his prior consent. In this way Garcia Pena actively disobeyed Mr. Madero's order.[57]

As Huerta recognized the full extent of his power as Commander in Chief he saw an irresistible opportunity. He had not been an active participant in the conspiracy of the generals although he approved it. Now, he saw no reason to involve the other generals at all. General Reyes was dead, Felix Diaz and Manuel Mondragon were irrelevant. He could control the nation by himself, and in the process, exact revenge for the humiliation he felt when President Madero fired him. Intoxicating ideas.

On Monday afternoon Huerta saw General Ángeles in the capital and was heard to remark with disgust, "What does the president see in that Napoleonic popinjay to get him here so quickly?"[58] Huerta was displeased because he knew that Ángeles would quickly recognize the sham campaign he was planning to wage against the rebels in the Ciudadela for what it was, a distraction... like a squabble started in a crowd by thieves to draw attention from the picking of pockets.

Huerta's responsibility was to remove fifteen hundred to two thousand rebels from the citadel in the middle of the city. The structure was built decades earlier to serve as a fortress. Now unused for that purpose it was storage for munitions and renamed the Armory but was more often referred to by its old name, La Ciudadela. President Diaz had added windows that gave light and air to the building which made more pleasant but less useful as a refuge. There were several possible methods Huerta might have used to oust the rebels; He could have simply starved them out. But, he had more effective means at hand: General Felípe Ángeles, world-class artillery general, could have placed artillery shells precisely into the Ciudadela and quickly crumbled its walls. The walls were thick but not impenetrable by the modern weapons of 1913.

The cunning Huerta did not want to abandon the rebels in the citadel, they were useful to him as pawns. Therefore, he wasted no time in neutralizing the artillery skills of General Ángeles and the loyal troops that came with him from Cuernavaca. He positioned Ángeles at a distance and at an awkward angle from the Ciudadela, near the confluence of El Paseo de la Reforma and Avenida Chapultepec with the British Embassy in the line of fire; a position that presented a dilemma to an artillery commander who had been ordered to protect the British Embassy against damage. That dilemma could have easily been avoided by placing canons on the opposite side of the Ciudadela, the side away from the embassy.

Huerta performed three additional acts to sabotage Ángeles' mission and to undercut the defense the city. Ángeles guns functioned poorly; the sights of his guns were deliberately damaged. Second, the ammunition given to him was shrapnel not high explosives. Worse, and unthinkably cruel to fellow soldiers, he purposely set out to destroy troops loyal to the president. The most callous example was sending loyal Coronel Juan Castillo and his troop of 75 men to the corner of Balderas and Morelos where there was no protection from machine gun fire. They were slaughtered, as Huerta knew they would be.

Elegant residences lined the wide boulevards that led to the Palace. Because the area of the battlefield was concentrated in the center of the city the damage done to those fine homes was severe. During the first few days multiple shots were fired and the Ciudadela was hit once and the Palace twice, but as planned by Huerta many of the lovely homes along the spacious boulevards were destroyed and hundreds of civilians were killed. People were in danger whenever they ventured onto the streets. Bodies could not be retrieved. Cadavers piled up and had to be doused with gasoline and burned where they lay. People began to go hungry for it was impossible to go out even if food were being sold.

Ten days of recklessly aimed canon-fire brought death to every street and caused crises throughout the city. Was the damage done residences of civilians caused by Ángeles artillery? Military witnesses later attested that the random destruction in the city was not at all the work of Ángeles' batteries. Even those shells which over and under shot their mark due to damaged sights on his guns, were on the line of fire. The random firing was from others determined to use carnage to promote their own goals.[59]

The city appeared to be held hostage by rebel guns, but in fact the rebels were caged within the walls of the Ciudadela. After a few days some people began to perceive Huerta's fraud. José Vasconcelos asked in a cabinet meeting why they did not attack the Ciudadela directly and have that 'pack of rats' out of there in a couple of hours? "It is shameful, he said, that a few hundred men can hold a peaceful city hostage." The patriotic but inept Secretary of War, Garcia Pena, responded haughtily, "That is not my role. General Huerta has responsibility for the situation." Huerta however, continued to give excuses to the president.

Each day Huerta met with the president and explained in detail how his plan to remove the insurrectionists would soon succeed. Each night he allowed the Ciudadela to be resupplied with weapons, food, water, alcohol… even women.

What was the purpose of this brazen deception? Huerta wanted the world to judge Madero's government incapable of controlling the situation. He planned to force President Madero to abdicate his position and leave himself the obviously capable leader of Mexico.

On February 15th, Pedro Lascurain and a group of nine senators came to President Madero and asked him to resign. One of the senators, (a member of the conspiracy) said to the president, "in order to avoid foreign intervention and prevent greater evils, we urge you… to take the advice of your Chief of the Army (Huerta) and resign. 'It is the only thing that can save the nation.'[60]

President Madero responded. 'The country has elected me and I will die if necessary fulfilling my duty; and my duty is here." Concerning their fear of intervention, he showed them a recently received cable from President Taft of the United States, which described the false conduct of Ambassador Wilson. The cable said, "you will be alerted that reports had been given to disembark forces have been inaccurate." Madero added, "I see that you are demanding my resignation because senators appointed by President Diaz, not elected by the people, consider me an enemy and would gladly see me fall."[61]

On February 16th secret negotiations were held at a house in the Roma district belonging to a civilian, Enrique Cepeda. Huerta met with rebels and let them know he was ready to declare himself in public as against Madero. He hesitated he said, because he feared foreign powers might not give him diplomatic recognition.

Those negotiations led to what is known as the Embassy Pact, in which Ambassador Wilson shamelessly invited conspiracy leaders to meet at the U.S. Embassy residence. The meeting was attended by Felix Diaz, General Huerta accompanied by Lieutenant Colonel J. Mass, and others. When Diaz entered the room the ambassador enthusiastically cried out, "Long live General Diaz, savior of Mexico." [62] Ambassador Wilson plotted actively to remove Madero and implied falsely to the group that the United States would recognize a new government.

Ambassador Wilson believed the military insurrection to be a true evaluation of the situation. He knew that solid men of Mexico were backing the coup. The interests of the country, as he viewed them, demanded it. Therefore, he deceptively asserted his personal opinions to be U.S. policy. Other examples of his interference are many. He made untruthful, exaggerated reports to the U.S. State Department about the situation in Mexico and directly threatened Madero with intervention from the United States.

In his official report of February 16th, German Ambassador Paul von Hintze stated that ambassador Wilson told him he would recognize any government able to restore peace and order to replace Mr. Madero's government. "I shall strongly recommend that my government grant recognition to any such government, he said."[63]

Ambassador Paul von Hintze, obviously annoyed, added to his report, "It needs to be made clear that the U.S. Ambassador fails to perform his duties as doyen of the diplomatic corps: not a single member of the diplomatic corps has received any news from him, (concerning the bombing and a cease-fire) however, he continuously claims to act in the name of the diplomatic corps."[64]

Huerta had unsolicited help from other sources. One was the press; journalists who had been strictly censored by dictator Porfiro Diaz, had complete freedom under Madero. Mainstream newspapers like El Imparcial, La Nacion and El Pais, rather than use their new freedom to practice professional journalism, turned to sensationalism and slander to demean the president. They published articles that called him insane for flying in an airplane and ridiculed his religious beliefs. In truth there was encouraging factual news they could have printed. For example, the monetary crisis of empty coffers was being solved by a loan from France at reasonable terms and there was progress in the war with Zapata.

By Monday morning February 18th, Huerta could see he had to act quickly. Public terror was at its height and his treason was about to be exposed.

CHAPTER SIX

The Last Days of President Madero

Huerta thought his meeting with the conspirators was secret, but a trusted friend of Gustavo Madero witnessed it. Jesus Urueta, lived next door to Enrique Cepeda on the Calle Napoli. Urueta knew Cepeda to be anti-Madero and when he saw Manuel Mondragon and other well-known opposition leaders enter the house, he became suspicious. When General Huerta arrived at the house, his suspicions about the meeting were confirmed. When the meeting broke up he went to his friend Gustavo with his evidence, convincing Gustavo that Huerta was disloyal.

The two men went to the National Palace to confront Huerta. Gustavo went upstairs to wait while Urueta went to find Huerta in a room where the two had met in the past. They chatted until nearly midnight, Urueta drinking coffee, Huerta drinking coffee laced with cognac, his favorite drink. At one point, Urueta excused himself and sent for Gustavo. Gustavo soon arrived armed and carrying weapons for his friend, Urueta. Together they arrested General Huerta, saying, "We know all about your treason." Huerta's protests were extreme, but unavailing.

Gustavo took Huerta upstairs to the Intendent's office, the office of General Basso, and indicated that Huerta was to remain under guard. Then he went further upstairs to his brother to report what had occurred. When President Madero understood what Gustavo had done, it was nearly two-o-clock in the morning of the 18th. He immediately went to the prisoner and allowed him to offer an excuse for his presence with conspirators. Huerta maintained, "it was an affair of the skirts," and nothing to do with his loyalty to the president.

The president accepted this explanation and gave Huerta twenty-four hours to complete the suppression of rebels in the Ciudadela. He reprimanded Gustavo for his action, attributing it to excessive loyalty and demanded he apologize with an *abrazo* (an embrace). Seemingly, that ended the accusation in a gentlemanly way. Huerta accepted the apology and requested the return of his weapons. Madero returned them with his own hands.

Huerta realized his explanation was weak, accepted only with the gravest reservations. He knew he must act quickly. Therefore, of necessity he accelerated the timetable by a few days, and decided not to allow Gustavo far from his sight. He considered him the most immediate threat to his plan.

President Madero held a meeting on the morning of the eighteenth with his cabinet and advisors to discuss removing the conspirators from the Ciudadela and ending the violence in the city. He sent for General Huerta to explain how he was addressing the problem and why the delays. The senators and cabinet members entered the conference room grumbling, impatient, and hostile because of the unending warfare in the streets. A few recognized the fraud of Huerta's ineffective actions. José Vasconcelos asked, "Why has the military not attacked the Ciudadela directly and had that pack of rats out of there in a couple of hours? It is shameful that a few hundred men can hold a peaceful nation hostage"[65]

Alberto Garcia Peña, the patriotic but inept Secretary of War responded defensively, "That is not my decision to make. General Huerta has that responsibility."[66]

Huerta assured the group of his loyalty for the "umpteenth time," and made clear to the senators that an attack would occur at 3:00 that afternoon; he was only waiting for General Rubio Navarrete to inform him that the artillery was ready. "By five-o-clock this afternoon the bodies of Felix Diaz and all who follow him will be hanging from posts in the plaza," he vowed.[67]

"You see," the president said with a smile to his advisors, "General Huerta has a plan that he is certain will succeed. There is no cause for alarm."[68]

Huerta did have a plan, but not the one he led the president to believe. His plan was to allow the city to be paralyzed, thus demonstrating to the world that Madero was unable to control the violent streets. This would force Madero to abdicate his presidency and leave himself the only capable leader of Mexico.

Huerta left the meeting and began to activate his treasonous plan. The plan was three-pronged, aimed at the president and his two strongest supporters, Gustavo Madero and Felípe Ángeles.

To eliminate General Ángeles, Huerta began by ordering a cease-fire. It seems probable that Ángeles was not informed of this. Across the city the staccato crackling of machine guns ceased, and one by one large guns became silent. "The guns of General Ángeles were the last to stop," said Alberto Pani. "I was listening to the noise of canons and thinking those are the guns of General Ángeles, when all of a sudden they stopped. I could not believe the silence."[69]

Within minutes Ángeles was summoned to the office of General Mondragon inside the Ciudadela; he was ordered to denounce the president. When Ángeles refused he was disarmed and arrested. He was taken to the Intendencia as a prisoner[70]

Huerta then went to Gustavo and invited him to a luncheon at the Gambrinius Restaurant across the street from the Palace. The luncheon was in honor of Francisco Romero and Augustine Sanguines, officers who were receiving promotions in rank. At first Gustavo declined, but Huerta insisted, claiming that the soldiers would feel slighted by his absence and added that he himself would take it as a personal insult.

The general was deceptively charming and pleasant during lunch. At one point a waiter called him to the phone, probably to confirm that the president was securely under arrest. He stood, excused himself, turned to Gustavo, and said, "I do not have my revolver with me, may I borrow yours?" Gustavo politely obliged.[71]

Following lunch Gustavo walked to the cloakroom with Adolfo Basso the Superintendent of the National Palace. There both men were arrested and taken to General Mondragon at the Ciudadela. Mondragon immediately condemned both to death. Basso was quickly executed by firing squad. That courageous man faced his executioners, ripped open his uniform jacket exposing his chest, and shouted, "Viva Mexico". Gustavo, however, was held in the Ciudadela until evening. There he was beaten severely then pushed staggering out the door and into the patio where a mob of more than 100 drunken soldiers set upon him, as ordered. His pleas for mercy were met by jeers and laughter. One in the crowd, plucked out his good eye with the point of a bayonet, blinding him. Then the jeering crowd prodded him and stabbed him with sword points. Someone in the mob held a revolver to his head and fired but the drunken hand was unsteady, and the bullet tore away Gustavo's jaw. He stumbled a short distance and fell at the foot of the statue of Morelos, hero of the War of Independence, Dozens of shots were fired into his body. His glass eye was pulled out and passed from hand to hand as a souvenir.[72]

Meanwhile, following Huerta's departure from the meeting in the National Palace, Governor Gonzalez Garza questioned if the president might not have the legal right to take command of the army. Madero considered the question and went to a library in an adjoining room to check precedents on which to base his opinion. Captain Garmendia, his former assistant now bodyguard, accompanied him while the others waited in the salon. As President Madero returned to the salon, lunch was announced and Madero asked his cousin Marcos Hernandez who was standing nearby, to join him. Marcos refused because he needed to go to his house to pack for a trip. Madero saw that Marco was unarmed and because he was concerned for Marcos' safety in the chaotic streets, he took his own weapon from his pocket and gave it to Marcos.

Suddenly, Lieutenant Colonel Riveroll and Major Izquierdo entered the Palace with about thirty armed soldiers in two ranks, accompanied by several civilians carrying machine pistols. They went directly up a flight of stairs to the Salon de Consejos.[73] Major Izquierdo ordered the troops to halt.

President Madero heard footsteps and voices and hurried toward the salon to inquire the meaning of the unexpected invasion, "Who gave you the order to enter here. What does this mean?" he asked Riveroll, indignantly. Madero had reached the door of the library that led to the Salon de Consejos, Gonzales Garza was near him and behind them both near the bookshelves, stood Captain Garmendia, his bodyguard.

Major Riveroll approached slowly with his weapon in his hand, turned quite pale, and said, "I am here to put sentinels on the balconies to prevent bullets from entering." Madero outraged, ordered the rude subordinate to leave the room immediately. Riveroll discarded all pretense and grabbed Madero roughly by the arm with his left hand, trying to force him out of the library into the ranks of soldiers and said, "The army is tired of maintaining a government of fools. You are under arrest in the name of the army."[74]

Madero was unarmed but he defended himself with his fists. He struck Riveroll in the face, which made the colonel hesitate. Then Captain Garmendia, without moving from the doorway shouted, "No one touches the President," and shot Riveroll in the middle of his forehead, killing him.

This was the signal for shooting to begin within the room; frightful confusion lasted for about five minutes. When Riveroll fell Major Izquierdo stepped out of the ranks and ordered soldiers to fire on the president. At the same time Captain Montes, assistant to the president, ordered the soldiers to lay down their weapons and about face. Marcos Hernandez moved between Madero and the soldiers. Some of the soldiers obeyed Montes who was threatening them with his revolver; others obeyed Izquierdo and fired in the direction of the president who was holding the frame of the door. Madero, serene and courageous to the point of temerity, stepped forward toward the confused soldiers saying, "Calm yourselves, boys, do not fire."[75]

Cepeda the civilian, took out his pistol and fired, shouting at the soldiers and threatening them with his weapon ordered them not to follow orders given by Captain Montes.

Rifles fired and Marcos Hernandez, Madero's cousin, fell mortally wounded. Captain Garmendia the bodyguard moved forward to the door, pushed the president aside and fired again, killing Izquierdo. Both rebel officers lay dead on the floor of the salon. Captain Montes repeated orders that were finally heard. He ordered the soldiers to present arms and march toward the corridor. The soldiers responded and obeyed his commands. Cepeda rushed headlong past them holding his bleeding right hand with his left. The index finger of his right hand was blown off, leaving him unable to continue fighting.

Ministers, who were civilians and unaccustomed to such scenes, swarmed to the closed doors or hid behind curtains and furniture Visitors and some members of the serving staff shouted, "Don't shoot!" at the soldiers.

Manuel Bonilla, Secretary of Development, seated in the Salón de Concejos, saw Riveroll fall but in the confusion that followed could not identify who was killed, he thought it might have been Madero. Calmly he stood, walked around Cepeda, and went to the corridor. Pino Suarez the vice president, followed him. Both men went down the stairs to reach the door to the street.[76] At street level Vice President Pino Suarez parted from Minister Bonilla and walked to the garages with Governor Gonzales Garza who also managed to leave the salon. Gonzalez Garza then went to the door leading to the street, but Pino Suarez thought he could leave with less risk by taking his automobile and lowering the curtains. By doing so he committed suicide. At the precise moment he climbed into the car Blanquet was there gun in hand to grab him by the neck and drag him out, saying "You are my prisoner." Pino Suarez could not defend himself. His back was toward his aggressor and he had no choice but to be led to the Intendant's room near the entrance of the Palace.

When Captain Garmendia reported to the president that the elevator was cleared of rebels and safe to use, the president decided to leave the Palace, find General Ángeles, and see if he might be able to save the situation, but Madero was told that rebels guarded the exits. Therefore, he stepped out on the balcony to assess the attitude of the soldiers below. The rurales[77] who had been in front of the National Palace knew nothing of the plot and were quietly eating when the president appeared on the balcony.

Madero called to the rurales saying he was coming down immediately and would need them to serve as escort. He did not tell them he was fleeing an attempted coup inside the Palace. Rather that he was going to lead them to the Ciudadela. At the end of his speech the rurales cheered, demanded weapons and prepared to ride with him.

Captain Garamendia raced out of the National Palace through an unguarded side door and down the avenue to the Imperial Hotel where General Ángeles had his headquarters on the Paseo de la Reforma. He was met by Lieutenant Colonel Miguel Bernard, chief of staff, who told him that General Ángeles had just left, summoned to Huerta's headquarters. The two men stared at one another for a moment as the enormity of the situation formed in their minds; the certainty that this was a treacherous coup. General Bernard was a patriot and an honorable man. He was asked years later why he had not ordered his men to stand against the traitors. his sad reply was "the code of discipline was a ruthless taskmaster."[78]

While Blanquet was occupied arresting the vice president, the president came down in the elevator and joined the rurales who formed to do him honors. The group was about to reach the street when General Garcia Hidalgo and a group of officers appeared with drawn guns. Those with Madero shouted, "Don't shoot, don't shoot." Madero impulsively ran.

At that moment, Blanquet left the Intendencia and saw the president fleeing across the courtyard. With great strides he reached Madero, grabbed Madero's arm and said, "You are my prisoner." The president, in spite of the fact that he was of small stature compared to the tall, well-built general, jerked away from his grasp and hit him in the face.[79] Officers who arrived to help Blanquet surrounded the defenseless president and despite his energetic protests. took him to the detention area, Ministers Hernandez, Madero, Lacurain, Vazquez, Tagle and Garcia were also apprehended, disarmed, and taken with the president.

In the Intendencia, Blanquet forced the president into the small room saying, "In here, in here, Señor." Blanquet gestured toward the other prisoners with his pistol, smiled fiercely and told his officers, "Bring those, too".

An officer pointed out that some ministers were missing, and soldiers were ordered to search for them. General Peña was quickly found in his office, arrested, disarmed and taken to detention. Only Minister Bonilla was missing.

The small room in the Intendencia where the prisoners were taken was separated from the quarters of Intendant Basso by a door. The division between the two rooms was opened making one larger room but there were no beds, no blankets, no food or water.

The prisoners waited several hours, at last Huerta entered the room, inebriated to the point of staggering. He directed himself to Madero and tried to speak: "Señor Presidente... But Madero interrupted, "What! Am I still president?" Huerta persisted trying to speak, but Madero angrily enumerated Huerta's previous treacheries and turned his back. Huerta then stretched out his hand to the cabinet members. Each refused his hand. When he reached the Minister of Justice, Manuel Vazquez, that gentleman crossed his arms, spit in Huerta's face, and said, "I do not give my hand to a traitor."

Disconcerted, Huerta left the room In the doorway he stopped, turned to his soldiers and shouted, "Soldiers, Long the live the president of the Republic!" He struck his chest with his fist, gave a defiant look into the improvised prison and left.

Nothing more occurred until after seven o'clock. Then one by one the cabinet members were taken out and freed after they swore under threat of death to accept the coup and not conspire against the usurpers. By nine o'clock there was no one left in the room but Minister of War, Garcia Pena, President Madero, Vice President Pino Suarez, and Felípe Ángeles.

A few visitors were allowed into the room for brief periods. Cuban ambassador, Manuel Marquez Sterling, a decent civilized man, came and stayed with them through the night. While political efforts to free them whirled outside the palace, inside the captives were left with their own depressing thoughts. Pino Suarez predicted, 'they will kill us, but they cannot kill Ángeles.

When the Cuban Ambassador, learned of Gustavo's murder, he realized there was no time to lose. He contacted Ambassador Wilson, doyen of the diplomatic corps, and requested that he urge Huerta to allow Marquez Sterling to make available passage to Cuba where the president and his family would find sanctuary. Ambassador Wilson replied, "You are free to make your request to General Huerta, as is any other ambassador, but do not do so in the name of the entire diplomatic corps."

While Marquez Sterling was trying to save the president through diplomatic means, Señora Madero also sought help from Ambassador Wilson. In his presence she pleaded that he save the lives of her husband and the vice president, but he coldly dismissed her request saying that it was not possible for him to interfere in the internal affairs of Mexico. This was the same man who cheered on the conspirators, met with them and encouraged them to believe that the United States would recognize the government of Huerta.

Ambassador Marquez Sterling, arranged sanctuary for President Madero and his family in Cuba. He also arranged for the "Cuba" to be made available to take them to exile in Cuba. The ship was at anchor at the port of Vera Cruz. He obtained assurance of safe passage from Huerta for the family to travel. A train to the port was scheduled to leave the following evening at nine o'clock pm.

When Madero first heard of the plan of exile he refused to go unless Gustavo went with them. He had not yet been told of Gustavo's death. He demanded that Ángeles be his escort. After prolonged negotiation Madero was at last convinced to resign when he was told that all his conditions were met including the release of Gustavo. He was assured that his resignation would not be given to the Senate until he was on the ship in Veracruz. He handed his resignation to Pedro Lascurain who released it immediately to the Senate. At that point the mantle of presidency fell upon Foreign Minister Lascurain himself. For one hour he served as President of Mexico, the briefest presidential reign in the history of Mexico. He completed his only official duty when he appointed Victoriano Huerta as Foreign Minister in his place. Then he himself resigned.

The following day the prisoners were notified that the train had been delayed until 5:00 in the morning. That was the hour at which President Porfirio Diaz left the city when he was exiled to Paris. But, as Ángeles suspected, the train would not arrive.

On the afternoon of February 22nd jailors brought three army cots to the makeshift prison, implying a longer stay. By this time Madero knew of Gustavo's death but bore his grief in silence. At about 10:00 pm lights were turned out. The cot of Pino Suarez was directly in front of the sentinel, that of Ángeles was to the right, and that of President was on the left. Madero covered his head with his sweater and wept silently for his brother.

Twenty minutes passed, lights went on in the room and an officer named Chicharro, entered. With him was Major Francisco Cárdenas who ordered President Madero and Vice President Pino Suarez to get dressed and come with them. Alarmed, Ángeles asked, "What is this? Where do you think you are taking us?" The two officers avoided answering the question directly, but Ángeles insisted in the imperative tone of a general to a subaltern. "Come, explain yourselves! What is this?

"We will take them out of here…stammered Chicharro…to the Penitentiary…Them, not you, General."

"Why was I not notified of this," the President asked, traces of tears still on his cheeks?

"Are they going to sleep there?" asked Ángeles.

Cardenas nodded.

"And why have you not ordered their beds and belongings moved?"

The officers tried to evade the questions but at last Chicharro grunted… "We will send for them later."

Ángeles embraced Madero, 'Goodbye my president,' he said. He had no doubt that they would never see each other again.[80] Separate automobiles took the two men to the penitentiary. Once inside the walls Madero and Pino Suarez were ordered to descend from their cars and were executed by shots to the backs of their heads. *Ley fuga*, (shot while trying to escape), was the official explanation; a transparent deception accepted by no one.

Left alone Ángeles made his way out of the Palace, overcome with grief and deep dread, too numb to notice the chill in the air. He walked the quiet predawn streets of the city to the home of his friend Manuel Marquez Sterling to pour out his grief to the Cuban ambassador. "What took the heart out of a man, he said, was to find that the sights of my canons had been deliberately damaged and to know that the guns I faced were guns of my friends. Poor Castillo sent to Balderos to be slaughtered…what have we done? God forgive us all."

CHAPTER SEVEN

The Huerta Regime

He is no drunkard now of wine,
As he was then:
He warms him up with a richer cup—
The blood of murdered men.

~Graves, Robert. I Claudius.

February 22, 1913:

Victoriano Huerta spoke from the balcony of the National Palace to a crowd below: "Mexicans...brothers, there will be no more cannonading. Peace has come!"

The *zocalo*, the enormous central plaza, erupted with cheers of relief and joy; bells of victory rang from churches across the city. The Huerta regime had begun. General Huerta assumed power and notified the world at large. In a letter to President Taft, he stated, "I have overthrown this Government. The armed forces support me, and from now on peace will reign".[81]

Each state governor received the following letter: "Today at 11:10 p.m. I have received by law the provisional presidency of the Republic by vote of the Congress of the Union. I have the honor of informing you for your acknowledgment signed, V. Huerta".

It was a simple informative message, nothing more than a polite request, yet every governor understood fully the ominous threat it carried. Most of Mexico's governors accepted Huerta's take-over immediately and complied with his demand for written acknowledgment without objection. Only a few governors in Mexico's northern states refused; Sonora, Chihuahua, Colima, San Luis Potosi, and Sinaloa stood apart and became the nucleus of resistance.

At noon the day that President Madero was arrested, soldiers swarmed through the offices of the National Palace to find and arrest members of Madero's cabinet. Manuel Bonilla was the only member of President Madero's cabinet to escape. At his first opportunity he walked calmly across a patio. At the door a custodian respectfully indicated that no one could pass. Without objection Bonilla went through another patio where soldiers were peacefully eating and singing while their women made tortillas. There was nothing as yet to indicate the tragedy taking place a few meters away. Soldiers who searched the National Palace were from varied battalions...the 29th, the 20th and dragoons. There was little or no coordination of their duties.

The minister reached the main gate still calm and not receiving an order to stop, proceeded into the street.[82] He walked to a house nearby and made phone calls. He was taken to his own home nearby where he picked up travel bags that had been prepared, and was driven to the house of his friend, Parra in Tacuba. There he hid during the long afternoon hours. Parra provided a partial disguise, a military cape. When it grew dark Bonilla left the relative safety of Parra's house and wrapped in the cape, went to the railway station. He took a train to the west-coast where he planned to go north to Nayarit or Sinaloa. He felt sure he could find support there.

He interrupted his journey by stopping in Guadalajara to explore the attitude of Governor Lopez Portillo y Rojas, governor of Jalisco and met with J. Trinidad Alamillo in Tepic. Alamillo deceived him by saying he would not support Huerta, when in fact he did. Bonillo continued his way north and he arrived in Manzanillo at noon on March 1. When he stepped from the train he was surrounded by 20 or so local police all with guns pointed directly at him. They had been alerted by J. Trinidad Alamillo to watch for him. Bonilla had no recourse but to go with the police to the Municipal President, the mayor, to be shot. A firing squad had assembled by the time Adolfo Stoll, the German consul was able to find a way to remove him from the authority of the Municipal President. Bonillo was then taken to Mexico City under a guard of 20 or 30 soldiers. In Mexico City the authorities contacted Huerta for instructions and Huerta ordered Bonilla taken before Alberto Garcia Granados, Secretary of the Interior, who had instructions. Garcia Granados was dining at his home when Bonilla arrived. Garcia Granados was a perfect gentleman, said Bonilla, who treated him politely and remembered that only a few days earlier Bonilla had saved his cousin, Jose de Landero, from execution. Garcia Granados prevented his execution by placing Bonilla under a kind of benign arrest requiring only that he present himself each morning at rollcall.[83] It took several weeks for Bonilla to escape and cautiously make his way to Nogales where he was welcomed by his friends.

Huerta was in a peculiar position when he took control. He had no support system. He rose to power without a political party; his army officers were divided between the privileged old guard and the enthusiastic young officers trained by Ángeles. Even the support of remaining conspirators such as Mondragon and Diaz, was conditional. Huerta had no previous political experience and his regime was founded on deceit and treason; however, he did have one asset, a shrewd understanding of fear, which he applied lavishly.

When Governor Maytorena of Sonora received news of the murder of President Madero, he immediately sent his lieutenant governor, Ishmael Padilla, on a secret mission to Chihuahua, Coahuila, and Jalisco in order to discover the military strength of each. All these states supported Madero. When Padilla reached the state of Coahuila he found Governor Carranza in a meeting with old friends Encarnacion Davila, Miguel Cardenas, and Enrique Arizpe who now represented the Huerta regime. Carranza was about to sign the acceptance agreement. In fact, The U.S. consul Phillip E. Holland had already informed the U.S. government of Carranza's acceptance. Padilla immediately demanded to speak to Carranza and managed to convince him to change his mind and stand against Huerta. How Padilla brought about the change of heart is not known but Davila, one of Huerta's representatives, wrote later that it was Padilla who caused the change.[84] Padilla was to visit Jalisco the next day, but he never arrived. Somewhere between Coahuila and Jalisco he disappeared and was never heard of again. Maytorena later speculated that he was taken to Mexico City and executed by Huerta[85].

Each northern governor received threats from Huerta that their property would be confiscated, they would be arrested and executed if they did not sign letters of acceptance. These were not idle threats. For example, on February 22nd Governor Abraham Gonzalez of the state of Chihuahua was arrested and held. Abraham Gonzalez did not command troops in the revolution of 1910, but his service to Madero was even more valuable. It was he who recruited Pasqual Orozco and Pancho Villa to the revolutionary cause. His position as governor gave him immunity from arrest. But with guns of his enemy aimed at his head he signed the dictated letter of resignation. The Legislature accepted his resignation and named General Rabago interim governor until elections could be held. On March 6th a detail of three officers arrived from Mexico City with an order from General Huerta to transfer the prisoner quietly. To avoid calling the population's attention General Rabago arranged for the prisoner to be removed at 11:30 that night. Major Benjamin Camarena, Captain Hernando Limon and Lieutenant Federico Revilla took Abraham Gonzalez to the railway station. The station was quiet and nearly empty. The small group entered a special Pullman car and the train left the station without lights. Forty miles south as they neared Bachimba Pass, Major Camarena signaled the train to stop. He ordered the engineer to proceed a few miles without them, wait thirty minutes and then return. Major Camarena ordered Gonzalez to step down from the Pullman car and the train pulled away leaving them in the silent blackness of the desert night.. Without delay Camarena shot Abraham Gonzalez to death. His men dug a shallow grave beside the tracks. The popular story about the governor's death was that he was shot and his body was thrown beneath a moving train to make the death look accidental. Historian William H. Beezley makes a convincing argument against that theory in his biography of Abraham Gonzales.[86]

When Governor Maytorena heard the account of the murder of his ally, Governor Abraham Gonzalez, he realized he too was in immediate danger. He requested a leave of absence for the 'sake of his health' and went to Tucson, Arizona. On March 7th from Arizona he wrote a letter to Secretary of State William Jennings Bryan pleading that the United States not recognize Huerta as president of Mexico. He wrote, "Sonora, Coahuila, Durango, Campeche, Yucatan, Morelos and Chiapas, states of Mexico are in armed opposition to the military usurpation of the dictator, General Huerta, and five more states are partially armed…" [87]

President Woodrow Wilson, a pacifist, refused to recognize Huerta on the grounds that he was an assassin and a dictator.

Governor Maytorena was pressured to recognize Huerta. He was visited in Tucson by Huerta's peace commissioner Esteban Maqueo Castellanos who carried a letter from Senator Alberto Morales asking him to stop his resistance. General Celso Vega wrote Maytorena asking him to come to Mexico City, giving promises of safety. Maytorena replied that he was too ill to travel. General Mondragon, Secretary of War and the murderer of Gustavo Madero, wrote that if he continued to resist all his property would be confiscated and he would be executed. General Huerta himself, wrote offering amnesty and added that if he did not accept he would be designated a traitor and treated accordingly. Maytorena was truthful when he claimed that he left Mexico for reasons of health. He also left his state in order to gain time to organize the resistance, time that he did not have while in his office in Hermosillo, because a federal army was garrisoned a mere thirty miles away. An order for his arrest could be carried out within hours.[88]

Within a month, on March 19th Governor of the state of Sonora Jose Maria Maytorena received a letter from Governor Carranza of Coahuila saying that in the name of unity he was going to create a revolutionary plan whereby he would be named supreme chief of the constitutionalist movement. When the Constitutionalists achieved their victory, he would take executive power until elections could be held. He promised that he would soon send a copy of the plan. He hoped that he would have the support of Maytorena. The plan included four points: 1) no recognition of Huerta as president of Mexico; 2) the organization of an army proclaiming Carranza as First Chief of the Constitutional Army. 3) V. Carranza will be the provisional president of the republic when the Constitutional Army takes Mexico City and 4) the provisional president will call national elections as soon as peace is established. All powers would be turned over to elected officials at that time. At the Guadalupe Ranch in Coahuila, on March 26, 1913, *The Plan of Guadalupe* was signed and accepted as the foundational document of opposition to the regime of Huerta. Unfortunately, the time limit established for the provisional government to be turned over to elected officials was sufficiently elastic to cause painful divisions and more bloodshed in the future. The condition 'as soon as peace is established,'… became, 'not yet'.

A few state militias were successful in minor skirmishes against the federales, but Governor Carranza fought losing battles against federal troops in his state of Coahuila. At the end of August, he fled Coahuila with 110 men, crossed the rugged Sierra Madre mountains on horseback, travelled through the state of Durango and reached Sinaloa. On September 12, Governor Felípe Riveros of Sinaloa informed Governor Maytorena, of Sonora of the arrival of First Chief Carranza and the poor physical condition of all in his company. Maytorena wired back to to give Carranza anything he needed, including underwear, uniforms, hats, shoes and horses. He gave Carranza $10,000 pesos, of which $2,000 was for his personal expenses. Maytorena met him with open arms in Sonora and. put all elements of the Sonoran government at his disposal. Carranza and the group continued to Hermosillo where they received a gala reception and set up resistance headquarters in the city of Nogales in the state of Sonora near the border of the United States.

Meanwhile, Huerta continued his campaign of terror. Rafael Cepeda, governor of the state of San Luis Potosi was murdered on the steps of his own home, and Governor Alberto Fuentes, of

Aguascalientes, was forced from his position.[89] The states of Chihuahua and Sonora were left as the focal point of the resistance.

From February 9 to February 18, 1913, the period known as the *Decena Tragica,* the Tragic Ten Days, the entire population of Mexico City was terrorized by open warfare. Although artillery rounds ceased to fall in Mexico City after Huerta seized power, terror still reigned. Now however, violence was directed specifically at Huerta' enemies. Snipers from rooftops executed those who openly opposed him. Others were found dead in roadside ditches, still others simply disappeared, as had Ishmael Padilla. Police searched homes at any hour; senators were jailed and shot; journalists who yesterday were free to write whatever they chose, were silenced by censorship as they had been by the dictator Porfirio Diaz. Members of the Madero family sought refuge in the United States or France, and cabinet members scattered.

In late September, Dr. Belisario Domínguez, a federal senator from the state of Chiapas, wrote a speech to be delivered to his fellow senators condemning Huerta's ascension to power through means of the assassination of their democratically elected president. He pointed out the obvious fifty percent depreciation of Mexican currency, the gagged press, villages cruelly leveled, and he called his fellow senators to repudiate Huerta as a "bloody and ferocious soldier who does not hesitate to kill when obstructed." The senate president refused permission for him to deliver the speech on the grounds that it contained no concrete proposal. Although undelivered the speech was widely circulated. Huerta ordered the senator arrested. He was dragged from his room at the Hotel Jardin, taken to a cemetery in the suburb of Coyacán and shot. His body was dumped into an open grave. Amazingly, there was no official reaction to his murder; the Senate continued sheep-like to follow Huerta's orders.

Unlike the Senate the lower house, the Chamber of Deputies, was made of sterner stuff, they demanded an investigation. Huerta ordered them to stop interfering with executive power. But the deputies remained firm and appointed a commission to carry out an investigation. Huerta's reaction was decisive, he sent troops from Blanquet's 29th Battalion (the same battalion that spearheaded the coup in Madero's office) to surround the Chamber of Deputies, From a list of one hundred and ten opposing deputies eighty-four were arrested and imprisoned. A fortunate few escaped and went into hiding or had already left the capital to join resistance groups in other parts of the country. Soon Huerta dissolved both legislative bodies. He also closed the courts. By October he controlled all three branches of government: executive, legislative, and judicial.

Felípe Ángeles found himself in an unacceptable position; he still held the rank of general in the federal army, and that army was loyal to a despicable traitor. How could he remain in the army and serve a government of assassins? However, to leave would be considered treason because he was legally and morally bound to that military. He held Huerta, Mondragon, and the cabal of conspirators guilty of the murder of his friend President Francisco I. Madero, as well as destruction of Mexico's new-found democracy. He felt deep shame for the role his beloved army had played in the vicious overthrow.

Huerta was in an equally difficult situation concerning General Ángeles. The brigadier general was a 'scorpion in his bosom'. He knew Ángeles would remain loyal to Madeero, their close friendship was well known. The fact that Madero ran to Cuernavaca when the *cuartelazo* (barracks revolt) began, rather than to Blanquet at Toluca, a closer post, was damning. He realized that Ángeles was revered, nearly worshipped by his students, the cadets and his ex-students, the young officers of the federal army. He also understood that without a doubt Ángeles would join the revolutionaries who were already active in the north. Huerta was not free to execute or assassinate Ángeles as he had other enemies because of international opinion plus the respect with which Ángeles held within the army. Yet, Ángeles remained a potential threat to his power. Huerta had a dilemma on his hands. His first solution was to fall back on the traditional method of handling disruptive federal officers, the golden exile. The day following the murder of the president Madero, Ángeles was ordered to appear before General Mondragon the new Secretary of War and was appointed the Mexican attaché to Brussels, a city where Ángeles was highly regarded. Huerta and Mondragon believed Ángeles would agree to serve there.

On March 2nd however, Huerta reversed his decision. He had the good fortune to discover a plausible reason to put Ángeles in jail and so eliminate the annoyance of his presence in public while simultaneously bringing discredit on his character. Ángeles was arrested for the supposed killing of a child. The plan was to keep Ángeles in prison indefinitely. Four months later a trial date had not been set.

Fortunately, General Ángeles had two powerful supporters, each of whom hoped to use him for their own agendas. One was the American ambassador to Mexico, Henry Lane Wilson, who did not object to the execution of Madero or Pino Suarez, but did object strongly to any action against Ángeles. The other was Manuel Calero, a conservative politician, who like Ambassador Wilson supported Huerta's coup, but wanted the presidency turned over to someone else, namely himself. Those two men along with other supporters of Ángeles insisted that a date be set for a hearing or trial that would bring an end to Ángeles' incarceration.

Calero defended Ángeles at his hearing and in examining the charges determined that the child in question was an eighteen-year-old, named Francisco Medina. He was the son of a businessman and the nephew of the governor of the state of Mexico. The young man arrived at Ángeles' artillery site in a chauffeur-driven automobile wearing a jacket and tie with his shirt collar reversed like a priest. He carried the card of his English professor, John Hubert Cornyn. Medina was a perfect example of an upper-class university student indoctrinated into rebellion against President Madero. Self-righteously, he believed himself a courageous patriot. Medina came to the site of Ángeles canons amid a battle and harangued the soldiers to dessert their duties, a treasonable offense. If Ángeles had ordered him to be shot it would have been the correct action. However, that was not what happened. Ángeles was not involved in the incident at all. This finding left Huerta in an awkward position. But Calero quietly began to seek a face-saving solution. He persuaded Huerta to send Ángeles to Europe on a military research mission. The mission was vague, and Ángeles was provided no funds. Huerta agreed, but insisted on one condition: that Ángeles must not set foot in any country before he reached Europe.

Meanwhile, now released from prison, General Ángeles was in an even more precarious position. Within prison walls under supervision there was some protection against Huerta and his henchmen. Out of prison there was ample opportunity for him to become the victim of an accident, or simply disappear. He was a marked man. Therefore, friends took him and his family to a secret place within the city to hide until arrangements could be made to smuggle him out of the country.[90]

In Cuernavaca life which had been improving under Ángeles' benevolent command, began to deteriorate. To the horror of local citizens, Huerta reappointed General Juvencio Robles to replace Felípe Ángeles as military commander. General Robles immediately reverted to genocide. Rosa King lamented her personal horror at watching her own heart become callused at the daily sight of bodies mummifying in the dry mountain air.

All who were able to leave Cuernavaca left, and international businesses recalled their people. But Rosa King, owner of the Bella Vista, could not leave; she remained with her hotel, her only financial asset. After months of anxiety she decided to go to the capital to find out what might remain of her future in Cuernavaca. She was able to speak personally to General Huerta. He gave her assurances of her safety.

Before returning to Cuernavaca she tried to find her friends Felípe and Clara Ángeles. That proved to be far more difficult.[91]

She asked, "And what of General Ángeles"? "No one knows," was the reply. "He was released from prison and disappeared. Perhaps he is in hiding, perhaps he is dead—the victim of another unofficial execution." The city was full of Huerta's spies and snipers who dropped unerring 'stray bullets' from house tops onto his enemies She finally learned that Ángeles was alive in hiding, and she was taken by a roundabout way, to a small house on a quiet street. She was told she must not remain long lest she draw attention to it.

During their brief visit General Ángeles told her of his last days with his beloved president when they shared imprisonment in the National Palace. She could see the extent of his suffering. He looked pale and appeared to have aged years in the months since she last saw him. As she left, he faced her, laid his hand on her arm and said very gently and calmly, "The snipers will not get me. I shall live to come back". As they shook hands in farewell he said earnestly, "Senora King, please do not stay in the city. Take Vera and go back to Cuernavaca. You are probably being watched for Huerta knows of our friendship".[92]

It is not known who made arrangements for the departure of the Ángeles because intense secrecy surrounded events. It is known that his defender, Manuel Calero, loaned him money to pay for the passage and that of his family. Ángeles was not a wealthy man for unlike other generals he had never taken anything from his position except his salary. He left Mexico with empty pockets.

A ship flying a German flag, the Antonilla, carried the Ángeles family from Mexico. It sailed from Vera Cruz on August 29, and first docked at Havana, Cuba. Ángeles did not disembark because Manuel Calero warned him not to leave the ship until he reached Europe, because of Huerta's conditions.

In Paris, General Ángeles met with Miguel Diaz Lombardo. Diaz Lombardo was the Mexican Ambassador to France appointed by President Madero shortly before his death. Born in Mexico to an aristocratic French family who had resided in Mexico since the days of the French Intervention. His grandfather was one of Napoleon's generals. Diaz Lombardo was in Paris when Huerta took power and there he remained. He became leader of the Resistance in Europe.

It soon became apparent to Ángeles that the Mexican movement in Paris was terribly out of touch and as 'blind as it was energetic'. Ángeles met several times with Diaz Lombardo. He explained his goal to unseat Huerta and the illegitimate government in Mexico, reestablish the constitution of 1857 and preserve Mexico's democratic institutions.[93] Ángeles offered his services to the Resistance and asked nothing from the revolutionaries but $5,000 stipend to take care of his family and his $2,000-peso salary as a general. Diaz Lombardo, notified Carranza and the anti-Huerta forces in Sonora that Ángeles offered to join them. José Maria Maytorena, governor of Sonora, sent personal funds to bring Ángeles to Sonora. Ángeles left France from le Havre on October 9th on a ship bound for New York. He is listed on the ship's manifest as Felípe Ángeles, businessman.

CHAPTER EIGHT

Joining the Resistance

The suspicious Huerta knew of Ángeles' plans and requested a fellow passenger on the Antonilla, Francisco de la Barra, and one of Huerta's aides, to keep an eye on Ángeles. General Blanquet cabled de la Barra in Paris about Ángeles. "Inform me as to the whereabouts of General Ángeles."[94] The vague reply from de la Barra was: 'The last I heard of Ángeles he was in La Havre and will remain there to study materials'.

It is known that Ángeles left Le Havre dressed as a civilian on a steamship bound for New York. The ships manifest lists him as Felípe Ángeles, businessman.

Several young officers of the Mexican federal army who had been cadets at the Military College under Ángeles direction, were doing advanced studies in Paris when Madero was assassinated. The army they served had been loyal to President Madero, and now General Huerta had murdered their president while the army made no move against the usurper. They were trained by Ángeles in a code of duty and honor. Their loyalty was with the murdered president, Francisco I. Madero, but their federal army was now controlled by the assassin, General Victoriano Huerta. When they learned their respected professor, General Ángeles, was in Paris, they decided to visit him. The group was composed of José Garcia Salas, Major Federico Cervantes, and José Heron Gonzalez. Gonzalitos was Ángeles' aide in Cuernavaca. Major Cervantes was in Paris studying aeronautics in preparation of creating Mexico's first Airforce. They searched until they found Ángeles' residence and went there to discuss the matter with him. At the Ángeles house, the general's wife, Clara, informed them that the general had gone to England to enroll their son, Alberto, in school. That may have been a partial truth to protect Ángeles and his family from Huerta's henchmen.[95]

Huerta was not the only one interested in Ángeles' movements during those volatile months following the overthrow of President Madero. United States Secretary of State William Lansing asked the consuls at the border to notify him if General Ángeles crossed from the United States into Mexico. Lansing learned that Ángeles crossed the border at Nogales on the seventeenth of October.

True revolutionaries who fought with Madero and fled to Nogales to resist Huerta were elated by Ángeles' arrival because they were certain that with his military expertise they could defeat the federal army. The night that Ángeles arrived in Nogales they celebrated with a high- spirited dinner filled with toasts and glowing speeches of welcome. When words were demanded Felípe Ángeles rose, stood on a chair, and made an impromptu summary of their resistance and its aims that was so moving it left the crowd cheering. Carranza added General Ángeles to his cabinet as Secretary of War, which was appropriate considering that was the position Madero planned for him in his legitimately elected government.

Men who supported democracy continued to flee from Mexico City to escape Huerta's reign of terror and join the counter-revolution. This included men like Raul Madero, the president's brother, as well as prominent intellectuals Luis Cabrera and Francisco Escudero who were known as *Renovadores,*[96] and Madero's personal secretary, Juan Sanchez Azcona, and Alberto Pani, a sub-secretary. Cabinet member, Manuel Bonilla, arrived following his daring escape from Mexico City. The army of the counter-revolution was an army of idealists not peasants. Men from Mexico City who knew Ángeles personally understood full well that though it took eight months for Ángeles to present himself for service, circumstances conspired to make him such a latecomer. However, volunteers from Coahuila and men from Sonora did not trust Ángeles. Why, they wondered, did it take so long for him to support the resistance?

In Paris Angles was disappointed to find an enthusiastic but out-of-touch leadership. What he found in Sonora, the self-proclaimed core of resistance, was disillusioning. Perhaps he expected a military base, where troops were trained and battle plans were made, instead he found gentlemen in three-piece suits working on day to day matters such as regulating mail, customs, and immigration. With them were hundreds of telegraphers, stenographers, secretaries, chiefs of staff and political hangers-on. They filled hotels in Nogales to overflowing. The only military present in the city were rebel commanders who came to Nogales to pay their respects to Carranza, formalize their authority, and receive money and weapons. [97] Carranza exhibited little interest in defeating Huerta. He reveled in his position as leader of a government in exile.

Hotel Escobosa in Nogales, a gathering place so crowded by an endless arrival of volunteers that men were sleeping three to a room. Martin Luis Guzman describes it as a shabby, dirty place with the unique advantage of being within walking distance of resistance headquarters where Carranza held court. Each afternoon an honor guard announced Carranza's exit from his office with a flourish of coronets; a parade of people then followed him in the street, people who wanted to experience the glory of the First Chief. An uneasy spirit of competition prevailed in his entourage. Factions competed for his attention; a tribute that Carranza relished.

Like a medieval king, Carranza and his court visited from city to city; in each he and the elite of his entourage were photographed with local politicians who provided elegant dinners. He ordered Ángeles to accompany them. Ángeles tried to avoid being photographed but Carranza insisted. Carranza valued the international respect that the name of Ángeles provided to his movement. His artillery skills were irrelevant.

The inner circle dined regularly with Carranza. At each refined dinner guests listened with profound respect to rambling monologues overflowing with historical allusions that often fell into errors school children would find laughable.[98] Never for a moment did Carranza allow the direction of the conversation to stray from himself.

Martin Luis Guzman describes such a dinner conversation on an evening following a day of battlefield victories.

Carranza began to pontificate as usual. He stated as indisputable fact the superiority of an improvised and enthusiastic army over a scientifically organized one. Any trained soldier would call that heresy as did the quiet Ángeles. He waited respectfully until Carranza finished his arguments, then rose and gently but most energetically defended the art of warfare as something that can be learned and taught, with better results for one who has studied it. But Carranza, despotic in conversation as in everything else, interrupted his Minister of War brusquely with a bald statement which closed the matter. "In life General, especially in leading and governing men, the only thing that is necessary or useful is goodwill."

Silence prevailed at the table. No one dared to break it. At last Martin Luis Guzman filled the awkward emptiness, and said, 'Hell is paved with good intentions' seems to me a wise saying because those whose chief characteristic is goodwill are always taking on tasks beyond their strength,…I am an ardent believer in books and training and I detest improvisations and makeshifts, except when they cannot be avoided." His outburst produced not surprise but rather stupefaction. All knew that Carranza's benign patriarchal smile covered a deep displeasure that would never be forgiven.[99]

Ángeles did not come to his work unprepared. He spent four months in prison following every scrap of news available about the resistance in the north. His military jailer, an admiring acquaintance, allowed him news and visits with other political prisoners who were equally obsessed with events. From prison he could see that while rebels fought skirmishes with intermittent successes their troops were untrained, their leadership amateurish and most glaring was the lack of a comprehensive plan to defeat Huerta.

Ángeles' first action as Minister of War was to develop a strategy, a three-pronged attack. He organized three armies to move simultaneously toward Mexico City, the center of Huerta's power. One army, led by Pablo Gonzalez, fought its way south on the eastern region of Mexico. Another army moved south on the western side of Mexico led by Alvaro Obregon and the third, led by Francisco (Pancho) Villa, followed the railway from Chihuahua toward the capital.

The first wave of *Maderistas,* supporters of President Madero, who arrived from Mexico City were well received in Sonora and some were given positions, but as the trickle became a flood, newcomers experienced a distinct coolness. One hero of the 1910 revolt, Gabriel Gavira, remarked on the hostility that he and others met in Sonora. Gavira had barely escaped death from Huerta and made a circuitous journey to Sonora by way of Cuba. Yet, efforts were made by Sonorans to prevent him from entering the resistance. Sonorans made clear that credentials as supporters of Madero in 1910 were not sufficient to establish them in the resistance of 1913. Many who felt this lack of acceptance, became disillusioned and moved on. Alberto Pani took a job in Washington DC and Martin Luis Guzman went east to meet with Pancho Villa in Chihuahua.

The state of Sonora had a long history of inter-family political feuding. Since the days of French rule families had been divided by vicious political maneuvering for power that fueled bitter recriminations. Sonora was described to the U.S. Secretary of State as a political 'snake pit' of infighting among a dozen or so wealthy clans.[100] Citizens of the state of Sonora in the camp of the Resistance proved the truth of that reputation.

One man in particular was threatened by the arrival of Ángeles and irate at his appointment as Secretary of War. Alvaro Obregon was part of a Sonoran clan, related by marriage to the wealthy silver-mining family, the Almadas. He farmed a tract of land in the Mayo Valley. A year earlier when concerns of a coup against Madero were developing, Governor Maytorena saw a need to increase defensive forces in the state of Sonora. He offered a generalship plus $200 to any man who could raise an army of 250 men. Obregon decided to meet the governor's offer. He was popular with men, a natural leader and always short of cash. He raised an army, and he received the title of general. The army he led proved to be quite successful. He could claim to have driven Orozco's rebel army out of the state of Sonora.

As General Ángeles worked to plan and organize an offensive, a whispering campaign began among Sonorans. Gossips twisted the fact that Felípe Ángeles had served his whole career under the dictatorship of Porfirio Diaz, insinuating he was a reactionary *Porfirian,* a supporter of dictator Porfirio Diaz, trying to infiltrate their movement. Over the weeks, Obregon's resentment of Ángeles grew to suspicions. He decided to take his suspicions to Carranza. Obregon says in his book, *"Ocho Mil Kilometros",* I told him, "Senor, I hate to tell you this, but General Ángeles is going to betray you" and he went on to explain that Ángeles 'has a problem telling the truth'. Obregon then threatened to withdraw his own support of the revolution if Ángeles remained Secretary of War. Carranza caved to this blackmail and made Obregon Secretary of War. General Ángeles was demoted to sub-Secretary of War, under the supervision of General Obregon.

This began a distressing three-month period for Ángeles. His objectives and those of his leader were distinctly different. Carranza's goal was to build personal power, not fight battles, Ángeles' goal was to atone for the atrocity committed by Huerta and the federal army and return the nation to democracy. Ángeles undoubtedly felt the sting of demotion, but that was trivial compared to his frustration at being kept from the battlefield where his artillery training could be put to use. Instead he was ordered by Carranza to pose for publicity photographs. Ángeles described his frustration to a friend, "I am nothing more than an office boy."[101]

Two weeks before Ángeles arrived in Nogales, Pancho Villa and his Division del Norte took the city of Torreon. By brilliant use of deception and misdirection Villa outsmarted the federal generals, Castro and Munguia. Villa and his Northern Division was the only army that had consistent military successes. The main reason why Carranza had been unable to capture Torreon was lack of discipline. Other generals also complained that the men of the Division del Norte were undisciplined. Villa overcame that problem within a week. He had the ability to transform groups of men who had little military training and no tradition of discipline into a well-organized, highly disciplined whole. He did not hesitate to shoot any man or officer he suspected of cowardice or disobeying orders. Revolutionary peasants accepted this without protest; they recognized him as one of their own and they felt that he had a right to take such measures. Ángeles observed Villa's strategy of relentless attacks which demoralized the enemy. He recognized and respected the innate military genius of Villa and compared him to Bonaparte.

Can it be coincidence that a telegram arrived in the Carranza camp from General Francisco Villa requesting an artillery officer for his Northern Division? Did Martin Luis Guzman drop a hint that there was an artillery general available? When news of Villa's request reached Carranza's headquarters the frustrated Ángeles immediately requested a transfer and Carranza promptly agreed to it. He found Ángeles a poor fit in the group of sycophants that surrounded him.

The seemingly unequal partnership between Villa, an illiterate peon and Ángeles the most highly educated man in Mexico's military, was an instant triumph. Unlike others Villa did not see Ángeles as a threat but had great respect for him. In turn, Ángeles sincerely admired the marshal skills of Pancho Villa. Even in small ways he gave Villa the respect due a commanding officer. For example, while other leaders of the resistance spoke to Villa in the

Spanish informal familiar tense *tu,* as one would to a servant, a child or a family member, Ángeles never did.

Together Villa and Ángeles created an unstoppable army. By mid-June 1914, their Division del Norte approached its greatest test, the fortress city of Zacatecas, the last barrier on the road to the prize, Mexico City.

Villa's successes were cheered in towns and villages. As the Division del Norte moved south Villa became Mexico's most popular hero. This angered Carranza because he feared that if Villa were first to lead an army into Mexico City, he would be seen both domestically and internationally as Mexico's national leader. Villa must be delayed in order to allow one of the other armies to reach Mexico City first. The crafty politician began by asking substantial concessions from Villa before he continued south to Zacatecas.

Villistas (Villa supporters,) in Chihuahua published the newspaper, *Vida Nueva.* In it the editor, Manuel Bauche Alcalde praised both leaders enthusiastically, but according to Carranza, Villa received a greater share of praise. In order to allay the First Chief's fears that he had national ambitions, Villa dismissed Manuel Bauche Alcalde.

Villa was willing to go a long way toward conciliation with Carranza. Because of that he made a foolish concession about the rail center of Torreon. Villa depended on the railway for transportation. Troops and horses were transported entirely by trains. Horses rode inside railway cars and men rode on the roofs. A railcar was Villa's mobile hospital. He entrusted the important position of Superintendent of the Northern Railways System to the capable Eusebio Calzado

Carranza replaced Eusebio Callzado with his own man as Superintendent of the intricate Northern Railway System. It was an unwise compromise for Villa to accept that change. The railways were a critical part of his military strategy. But even those concessions were not sufficient to satisfy Carranza. Remnants of the federal army had retreated from Torreon to Saltillo, the capital of Carranza's home state of Coahuila, and to the smaller town of Paredon, nearby. Carranza wanted control of the city of Saltillo which was not on the direct path to Zacatecas.

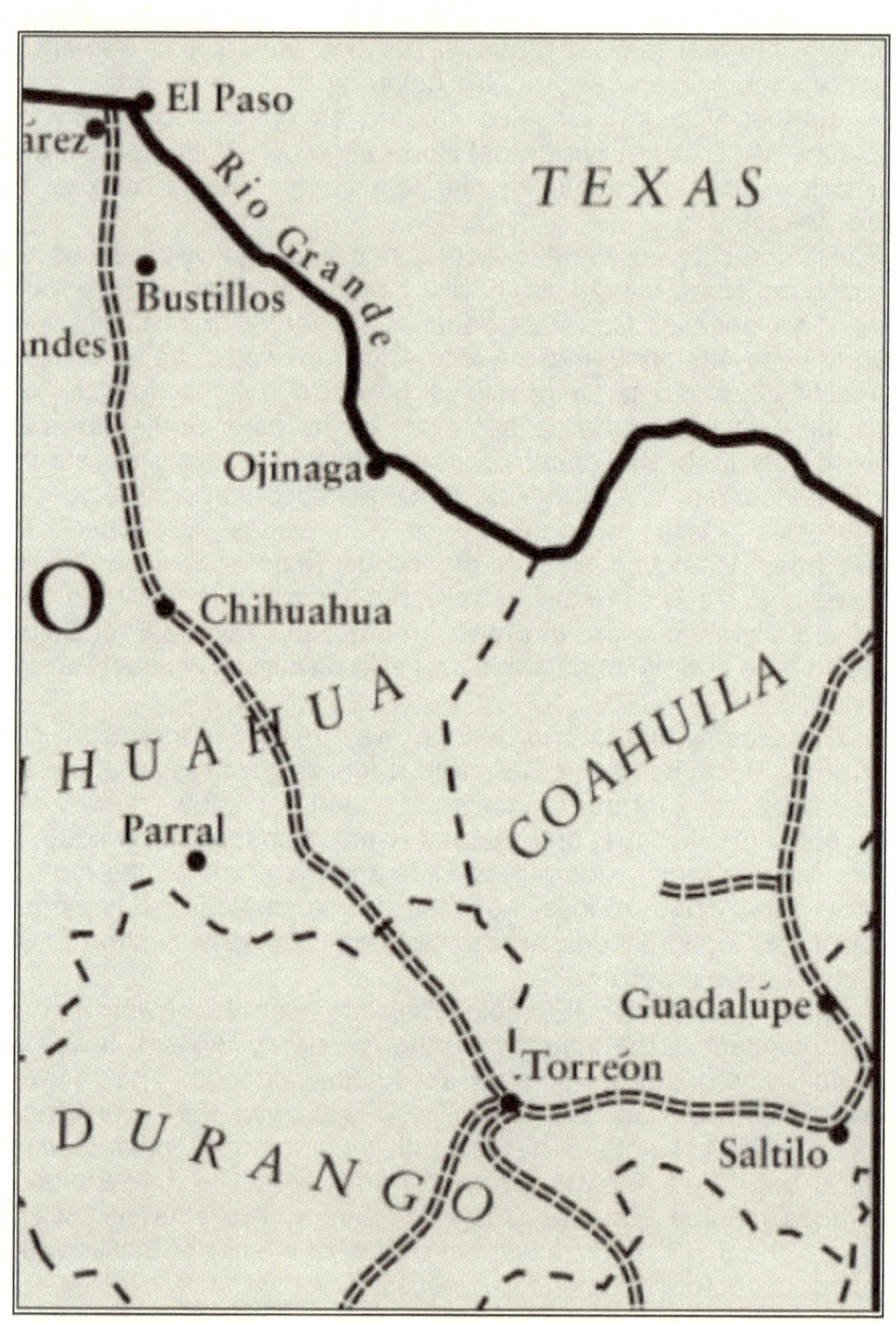
El Paso
Juárez
Bustillos
andes
TEXAS
Río Grande
Ojinaga
O
Chihuahua
HUAHUA
CHIHUAHUA
COAHUILA
Parral
Guadalúpe
Torreón
DURANGO
Saltilo

[102]Pablo Gonzalez, commander of the Army of the Northeast, was the logical one to capture Saltillo for he was much closer, but Carranza insisted that it be Villa. The more politically astute Ángeles understood Carranza's motives. A move eastward to Saltillo would not only delay Villa, but fighting against 15,000 federal troops would mean casualties that would weaken the Division del Norte. Ángeles warned Villa that going to Saltillo was a distraction, but Villa wanted to keep the peace. "Let's keep the old man happy," he said.

Federal commanders of 6,000 men in Paredon tried to delay Villa further by tearing up 20 kilometers of railway track near the town. But Villa, not to be deterred, disembarked his cavalry from the trains, and 8,000 riders rode around the damaged tracks to storm Paredon. The federal army lost 500 men and 2,500 were taken prisoner or wounded. Two federal generals were killed. Ten canons and 3,000 rifles were captured by Villa. The troops that were in Saltillo retreated rather fight. After the victory Villa and his troops marched into the city of Saltillo and made no effort to keep control of the city nor the surrounding area. Instead he handed the entire area over to Carranza, who set up his headquarters there.

On June 8th Villa sent Silvester Terrazas to Saltillo to negotiate a compromise. Villa hoped the concessions he had made would make Carranza open to talks. He tried to negotiate the disposition of haciendas and other confiscated properties and the issuance of paper money by Villa. However, the most important point to negotiate was control of the Northern Railway. Villa was dependent upon trains to allow him to advance to Zacatecas, the advance Carranza was trying to prevent. Carranza refused to concede even the least of these points.

Instead Carranza set up a new division called the Army of the Center, created specifically to move south to and capture the city of Zacatecas. To lead the new army, he appointed Panfilo Natera, one of Villas subordinates. In order to cause divisions within the Division del Norte he encouraged all revolutionaries who might differ with Villa to join the new army corps. As an additional insult to Villa, Carranza made Natera of equal rank to his former commander.[103] According to Carranza's bureaucratically inspired battle plan, Natera would capture Zacatecas. Pedro Alvaro and his Army of the Northeast would join Natera and together they were to march south from Zacatecas and occupy Mexico City, thus leaving Villa isolated in his bailiwick of Chihuahua. However, the plan failed. Natera attacked Zacatecas again and again. Each time he failed. Fortress-like geography combined with well-equipped federal troops were too strong.

It was obvious even to Carranza, that only Villa and his Division del Norte would be strong enough to take Zacatecas. But Carranza clung to his previous strategy to deny Villa any renown. Instead he ordered Villa to detach 5,000 of his troops and place them under

Natera's command. Villa tried to get Carranza to reconsider but Carranza was adamant.

At last Villa had enough, He exploded with a fury so great that those close to him feared for their own lives. He raged that he would march to Saltillo, surround the city and hang the old man. Villa's fury was intense because he could see that he had been deceived and he himself had allowed it. When asked by Villa if he should march on Saltillo his advisors, Felípe Ángeles and Roque Gonzalez Garza persuaded him that such an action would be a distraction from their real goal of reaching Mexico City and removing Huerta.

Villa explained Carranza's actions to his generals. Nothing Carranza could have planned would have been as effective at uniting the Division del Norte. Generals crowded into the telegrapher's office while Villa initiated a telegraphic conference with Carranza. Villa asked Carranza to reconsider his order. He pointed out that his men would be uselessly slaughtered, and the attackers would still be defeated, a not too subtle indication of Villa's opinion of Natera. He alone in command of a unified Division del Norte would be able to take Zacatecas, he stated. Carranza refused to listen to Villa's arguments and repeated the order to detach 5,000 troops.

That was too much for Villa. He responded, "Señor, I resign command of this division. Tell me to whom to deliver it".

Ángeles was unaware of what had happened until Villa called him into the telegraph office and told him to sit down. Without explanation he said, "See what you can do with these troops, General. I'm leaving." Ángeles knew that without Villa the Division del Norte would dissolve, momentum would be lost, and the demoralized federal troops would regain courage to resist. In the telegraph office worried generals waited for Carranza's reply. They agreed with Ángeles, they were facing disaster. When forced to examine the possibility of fighting under another commander they found it unacceptable. If there were generals who wavered or objected to Villa's leadership in the past this moment crystalized their thinking. Some still hoped Carranza would not accept Villa's resignation, Ángeles told them that was a false hope.

Carranza replied that he accepted Villa's resignation and ordered the generals to appoint one of their own as temporary

Commander in Chief.

Ángeles drafted a reply, a short but courteous message asking Carranza to reconsider his decision. Carranza refused. The generals then went to Villa and asked him to reconsider his resignation and Villa agreed. He became Commander of the Division del Norte once more.

When Carranza received their decision, he was furious and replied that he refused to accept Villa's renewed command, and he threatened to impose a commander without consulting them. The generals then unanimously signed a telegram to Carranza, drafted by Ángeles, that was much less respectful but stopped short of repudiating his leadership.

"We consider your measure a violation of the laws of politics and war and the duties of patriotism," they wrote.

> "We say further that among all those who defend our cause, General Villa is the chief with the greatest prestige, and if he should obey your order and retire, the people of Mexico would be right in blaming you and realizing your very great weakness, and they would accuse you of being the cause of a great loss. We say this and much more, Señor: We know very well that you are looking for the opportunity to stop General Villa in his action because of your purpose to remove from the revolutionary scene men who can think without your orders, who do not flatter and praise you or struggle for your aggrandizement but only for the rights of the people."

The generals ended he telegram by informing Carranza that they all would march south…to Zacatecas.[104]

The Battle of Zacatecas

*What could restore a moral order so violated,
nothing less than a sacrificial bloodletting.
La Bufa, became the Mount Moriah of Mexico,
the site of sacrifice.*

~Anonymous

G eneral Ángeles studied the theory of warfare at St. Cyr in France. He understood that action based on scientific principles win against an undisciplined mob of soldiers no matter how enthusiastic and courageous. However, much as he trusted his theories he had never put them into practice. His life had been spent in classrooms as a student or a teacher, never once on a battlefield. He taught that a battle was won or lost long before the first shot was fired. Reconnoitering the entire area carefully was the essential first step. He tried to visualize how the battle would begin and how it would develop. Would the lay of the land help or hinder him? Where was the enemy artillery placed? What would be the most difficult hurdle? From where might replacements come? Was there a means of retreat open for the enemy?

The following is the battle diary of General Felípe Ángeles: In it he records his observations of the battle. In them the reader can recognize steps of his theory put into action as the battle developed.

June 17, 1914

Early Wednesday morning we began our journey from Torreón to Zacatecas, less than 200 miles but it would take two full days. My division went in five trains; four carried my troops and the fifth carried my staff, provisions and workers.

The first train left at 8:00 o'clock, the others at fifteen-minute intervals; however, the fifth was delayed because of poor track condition. It could not leave until two o'clock in the afternoon.

The journey was slow. Several rain showers made travel miserable for my troops who had no protection, not even raincoats.

June 19, 1914

Friday morning, the 19th we arrived at Calera and disembarked immediately. Calera is about 25 kilometers from Zacatecas. The troops who had preceded me were waiting camped in the immediate area. Because of the good faith and confidence that the general of the Division[105] had granted me, I took the initiative to reconnoiter and distribute soldiers around Zacatecas in positions near where they would participate in the attack.

General Chao, who had just arrived, came to visit me in my car and showed me where his troops would be camping. He also promised me an escort of 30 men to reconnoiter toward Morelos, "I, myself, will accompany you, he said."

Three kilometers from Morelos we came across San Vicente, an abandoned *ranchito*. I sent some men to look it over. When we reached it, I divided the escort into three parts to explore further: the main body was directed straight ahead toward the hills in front; another through a deep gulley and on to some hills on the left, and the rest went toward Morelos.

Residents of this village and laborers in the fields that we were crossing, told us that they were fleeing from the enemy who had just come to Morelos, with the intention of burning forage and provisions; they pointed out silhouettes of mounted cavalry on the crests of the hills nearby and assured us that the shots we heard on the right were from the enemy.

Probably the enemy saw that we were few, perhaps they even counted us, for they decided to attack at a gallop firing shots against us.

We retreated slowly toward San Vicente observing the enemy all the while; when we reached a favorable place, we dug in and engaged in a firefight for about half an hour. The enemy retreated in order.

As soon as those in the camp at Calera heard shots fired, General Urbina sent the intrepid General Trinidad Rodríguez with his Cuauhtémoc brigade to assist us. They swept the enemy from the hills in front of us. We climbed there soon after.

From a high hill next to Morelos, we saw a beautiful new landscape. In the distance the chapel of Vetagrande clung courageously to the mountainside and reached toward the skies; a little to the right were high and mysterious hills full of excavations... mines or fortifications; perhaps the enemy was hiding among them. More to the right and at our feet lay a carpet of green fields strewn with villages and trees. At the bottom of the hill dogs were barking and, wonderful sight, enemy soldiers were fleeing from our soldiers who pursued them headlong firing their rifles with great enthusiasm, a few were trying to cut off their retreat.

"It would be good", I said to General Trinidad Rodríguez, "if your troops could stay in Morelos and send scouts to those hills in front of us".

I am going to bring artillery and position it in Morelos.

Major Barzán went into town to scout positions for the artillery while the rest of us returned to Calera. I ordered artillery taken to Morelos. Carrillo's group left soon after.

An officer came from General Monclovio Herrera to inform me that they had arrived and to ask me for instructions. I went to see General Herrera; I told him I had not received orders to take charge of the troops in Calera, and that perhaps General Urbina had that command; but I would advise him to go to Cienaguilla, a place that had water and forage and was not yet occupied by other troops, a place favorable for his attack, when he was so ordered. I had no knowledge of Cienaguilla other than what I had learned from my guide and by letter. I promised to visit him the next day to study the terrain for the usefulness of the artillery and to decide how many pieces I should send him.

The groups of Saavedra, Jurado and Luévano also left for Morelos.

A formidable downpour fell, and a strong wind began to blow. It was quite late when the three groups, my staff officers and I reached Morelos. I learned then that Trinidad Rodríguez had pursued the enemy beyond the batteries of Las Pilas and Hacienda Nueva, and that he had asked Carrillo's group for help attacking the enemy who had made a stronghold on the hill and the mines of Loreto.

June 20

I bathed in a miniscule tub.

General Pánfilo Natera came to greet me; he was mounted on a very small horse, but acceptable. We had breakfast together. He promised to accompany me with his escort and to guide me in today's reconnaissance mission.

Later we went to Vetagrande, a town once famous for its silver mines but now in sad condition, almost dead.

From the summit of the nearest hill, we saw a beautiful panorama. To the right was the valley of Calera and Fresnillo, very large and much lower with many villages that seemed to dissolve in the radiant light of the morning. In front of us, a portion of the city of Zacatecas, between the two hills of El Grillo and La Bufa, which were two formidable, fortified positions. Between the two hills, in the far distance, behind the visible part of the city, was the hill of Clérigos. Behind La Bufa, under some vaporous clouds that looked like bursting bales of cotton, was a mountain plateau made blue by distance. To our left was a creek-bed that began almost at our feet and ended near Guadalupe, a village that is out of sight, but that I could visualize being behind a small cone-shaped hill. In the same direction and further away, a lagoon appeared as a mirror in the morning sun, on whose edges are pleasant groups of houses. And between us and Zacatecas, two rows of hills, one toward El Grillo and the other toward La Bufa. Separating the two were the ruins of an adobe village that in other times had been silver mine called La Plata.

This spot is certain to play the most important part of the battle to come. I could not take my eyes from it. Little by little I headed for the future battleground; General Natera was close behind me then Colonel Gonzalitos, a discreet 100 meters behind: officers of the staff and their escort had dismounted, spread out, and were hidden on the other side of the high hill.

"It would be good," I said to the congenial General Natera, to bring our horses and move forward toward that deserted mine (the La Plata mine) and control it so we can see the battlefield better and more tranquilly.

When the escort took the road to the city, the canons on La Bufa sounded repeatedly and then I heard firing from a fight in the mine that was finally taken by the escort commanded by Major Caloca. That young man dropped out of Military School at Chapultepec last year and came north in search of me.[106] Sr. Carranza, however, ordered him to stay with General Natera[107].

After a thorough inspection of the area, we walked a little further down the creek-bed that ended near Guadalupe then returned to Morelos to eat. I gave orders to Major Bazán to go toward Vetegrande and set up the first two artillery groups where they could cover El Grillo and La Bufa.

About two o'clock I went to visit General Urbina in the (Morelos) Municipal building. Natera, Triana, Contreras, and other officers were with him. They had agreed that the troops of the last three generals mentioned as well as those of Banuelos, Domínguez and Caloca, would go to Guadalupe to take positions. General Natera told me that he was excusing himself from his commitment to accompany me on reconnaissance this afternoon. I informed Urbina that I am sending two groups to Vetagrande to place artillery by night in the spots I judge to be the most important part of the battle, and I asked him to send support troops to service the artillery. He sent me part of his brigade: the brigade commanded by General Ceniceros and a regiment from the Villa Brigade.

We dined well and pleasantly with General Natera and we agreed to meet at three o'clock in the afternoon to go and inspect the area around Cieneguilla, where the troops of generals Herrera and Chao were located.

An envoy from General Herrera came to Morelos to look for me and remind me that I had promised to go to visit him to study the terrain and see how best to utilize the artillery. Major Cervantes, Captain Espinoza de los Monteros and I, went to San Antonio, where the troops of Herrera and Chao had advanced. The enemy artillery from El Grillo hit the ground we were crossing near the railroad and damaged a locomotive going from Pimienta to Fresnillo.

An official message from General Herrera, who we were using as a guide said, "It is safer here. By not taking precautions some officer and a soldier were wounded. Do you see where earth has been removed? That is a mine. There are a lot of *federales* (federal soldiers) there. They are very good shots".

My horse Ney is no longer lame and even without stretching his legs his long stride and vigorous gallop were a delight.

We found General Herrera in San Antonio, inside a dark house full of officers stretched out on the floor. The general came out from among them with his usual good humor. "*Buenas tardes*, my general, we are leaving right now to explore the terrain and I am just waiting for my horse to be saddled. I will go on this one. Whose horse is this?"

We climbed a hill. "Careful, men, put your feet on the ground, (better walk) because they (the horses) make good targets from there."

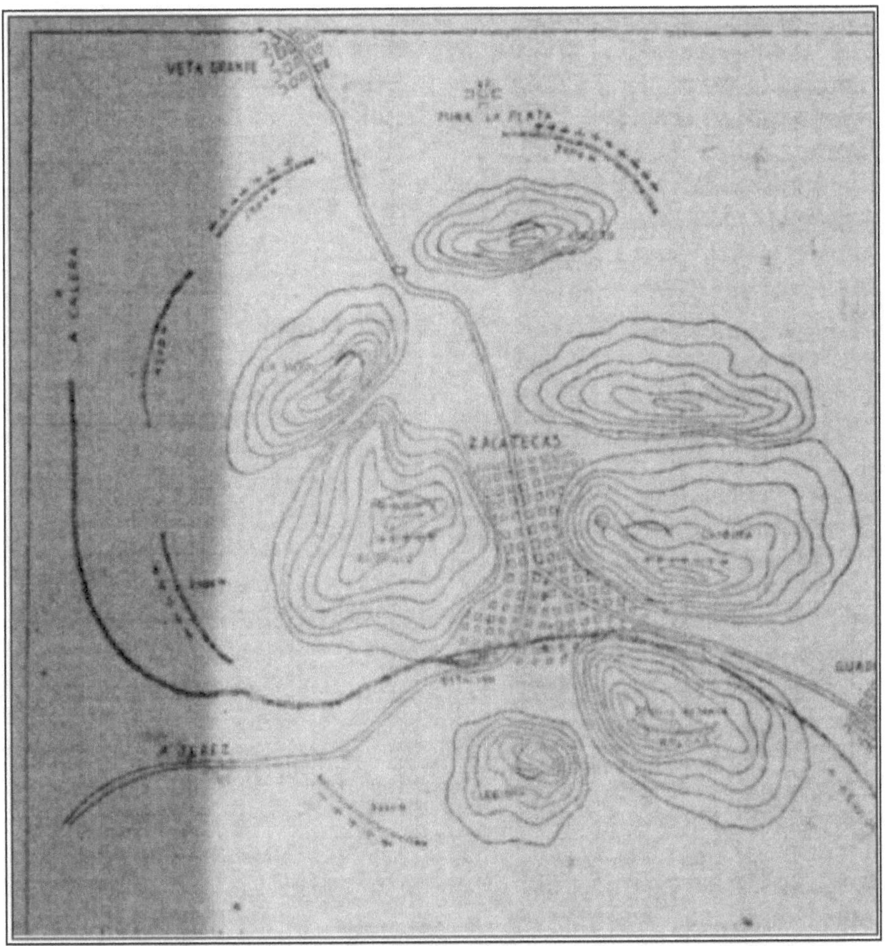

Figure 1 – Topographical map of Zacatecas drawn by Major Federico Cervantes. (Courtesy of Historical Archives of the State of Zacatecasl, Mexico).

We obeyed and walked to the crest of the hill; General Herrera remained on horseback.

In front of the small hill that we occupied was another valley, and then another larger hill that was infested by the enemy and dominated closely by El Grillo and La Bufa. On the right was the mountain of *Los Clérigos,* crowned by black points (the enemy lurking in ambush) and more to the right was the mountain whose top was the high plateau that I had seen this morning behind La

Bufa. There were black dots on that plateau as well. Were they friends or enemies? We did not know.

"Do you see that mine, my general?" they said to me. "That is El Rayo. And see those other houses, and the large corral? There are a lot of soldiers there; but send us a couple of canons and we will pound them until their tongues hang out. Wouldn't this be a good place to fire against those positions?"

"No, this is too far away," I answered. "I am going to send six canons that I have available, but don't place them here. At least place them on that hill in front of us, or better still over there, on the right side. The canons must be close so we can see clearly that they are hitting the enemy; and we must not fire when the infantry starts its assault. You know the artillery terrifies; when the canon roars, the enemy runs for cover and our infantry advances, and when the enemy dares to stick their heads out again our infantry is on top of them. The enemy abandons quickly. The enemy won't fire a shot at us.

We said farewell wishing to be together during the battle.

One officer accompanied us so that he could guide the way for the return of the artillery I would send.

Our return trip was quite different! It was a longer route especially for the horses. On the hill, La Sierpe, we heard persistent firing. From Zacatecas smoke rose to great heights. To me that suggested the federal garrison was going to abandon Zacatecas. I was informed that artillery could reach Guadalupe more quickly from General Herrera's position than from Vetagrande, and I thought that it would be better to send all of the third group to San Antonio, instead of the six pieces I had originally sent. If the *federales* retreated they would go by Guadalupe, and it would be necessary for General Herrera to have numerous artillery pieces in position in order to pursue them more effectively.

As we passed Las Pilas I gave orders to Major Carrillo to go immediately to San Antonio to be under the orders of General Herrera and support his attack.

We dined contentedly and slept happily.

June 21, 1914

As I bathed I was a bit concerned because I did not know if the troops that were to support the two groups of artillery set up during the night between Vetagrande and Zacatecas, were well and effectively placed and going to be effective.

I ordered Col. Gonzalitos to take his battalion from Las Pilas to Vetagrande to help protect the artillery and I went in a bit of a hurry soon after together with my staff officers.

We had reached Vetagrande when a messenger from General Natera delivered a written message asking what I knew about that day's attack and what mission his troops were to perform.

I answered him, also in writing, that I did not believe that the attack would begin that day: mainly, because General Villa had not arrived and he would have to direct the battle; and secondly because some troops had not yet arrived and it would be a military mistake not to employ all troops available, and third, because not all of our munitions have arrived and we must not start a battle without reserve munitions.

With regard to the mission of your troops: I told him, I think when they attack Guadalupe the mission must be two-fold: first, to prevent the arrival of reinforcements from Aguascalientes by destroying the train tracks and detaching troops to stop reinforcements; second, to stop the exit of the garrison from Zacatecas by way of the road to Guadalupe toward Aguascalientes by positioning troops in Guadalupe and its surroundings. Both groups must be nearby to give each other support.

In the narrow streets of Vetagrande there was an accumulation of service cars for the provisioning of the artillery. I sent to look for places to lodge my staff and to establish a hospital. A few minutes later we went up the high hill to see the positions the artillery had taken.

The battery of Captain Quiroz had been designated to occupy the top of that hill; his service cars were obstructing the road; the movement of the battery was very slow due to the steep grade that required a double team of mules. We dismounted. Up ahead we saw two canons; their maintenance crews were straining as they labored over the wheels but finally they placed the canons in their definitive positions. Generals Trinidad and José Rodríguez came to greet me with the enthusiasm usual just before combat commences.

On the side of the hill away from the enemy there were many horses saddled and loose. They were to support the artillery that was being positioned. The enemy was cannonading our battery hotly; the maintenance crews were shielding themselves by lying face down on the ground behind small mounds of stone and the gunners worked cautiously because the enemy artillery had made a few hits. In a careless moment one guncarriage rolled backward, slowly at first, then faster. Some gunners tried to stop it but without success. The carriage began to roll over rapidly and was heading in the direction of the horses. It was impossible to stop it and everyone felt anguish for the horses that could be killed; but fortunately, the carriage rolled to one side, bounced a few times and reached the bottom of the abyss.

In the distance, wrapped in the brilliant clarity of the day, an immense valley could be seen dotted with small villages and covered with trees.

On the other side of the hill, in the direction of Guadalupe and atop the ruins of the La Platera Mine, I could see five batteries with their gunners immobile behind plates of armor, Some were making trenches to provide better cover from the persistent fire of the adversary. The batteries had received orders to take position but not fire even though being fired upon.

Further to the right in the mine of the hill of Loreto, the enemy battled the brigades of Villa and Cuauhtémoc on their flank, who were spread out along the crest below us. Even further away, ascending the crest of La Sierpe, looking like the spine of a huge animal inhabited by a row of black dots; they were visible from where we were but hidden, except for their heads, from the side of Hacienda Nuevo and Las Piles where we had our troops.

The canons of El Grillo and of La Bufa thundered constantly and our stationary artillery were receiving enemy grenades. Directly across from our position, Chao and Herrera were being battered.

In the afternoon we set up a hospital in the lower part of our camp, visited the advanced batteries, and chose places to help the wounded.

It rained cruelly on our gunners who had no raincoats.

As we returned to Vetagrande, we heard the piercing cries of the gravely wounded and saw the dead stretched out in the patio lying on stretcher, faces covered with a handkerchief.

Someone reported to me the great destruction done by two shells, one from the enemy that had hit in the heart of the battery of Quiroz and another of our own that had exploded in the hands of a gunner as he put in the firing pin.

The Schneider-Canet canons would not return to their carriages after a few functional shots. Major Cervantes left on foot for San Antonio in the middle of the night, in search of Lieutenant Perdomo to repair the brakes. After an exhausting hike, Cervantes returned to Vetagrande at three in the morning with Perdomo.

June 22, 1914

I woke early concerned by the rains that had fallen on my soldiers, and about food service for the artillery that was not as satisfactory as I wished and wondering why the brakes on the Schneider-Canet canons were not functioning well; perhaps because the workers had loaded them badly and because projection charges of the projectiles were defective.

I advised Barzán to order an improvement in the food service. I spoke to Perdomo and Espinosa de los Monteros about fixing the brakes of the Schneider-Canet canons, and I ordered Major Ángeles to establish a first-aid station for the wounded.

I learned that the Zaragoza brigade had arrived in Morelos under the command of General Raúl Madero, and I left for that town with the object of bringing that brigade to Vetagrande; but, speaking with General Urbina, in Morelos, I learned that the Zaragoza brigade was on its way to another position and it would be Raúl's responsibility to visit the positions near Vetagrande.

Going along the road to the mine we ran into an officer who told us that General Urbina had modified the order for the Zaragoza brigade, in the sense that it would be outside the terrain occupied by the artillery, proving to me once again General Urbina's tactful efforts to keep everyone happy without prejudicing the service.

With Raúl I visited the battery of Quiroz from where I showed him the positions of all the canons. After lunch Raul went to inspect his troop.

I was walking over to inspect the artillery when Lieutenant Trucios let me know me that General Villa had just arrived and was coming to see us.

We saw him, friendly and enthusiastic as always, mounted on the spirited little horse of General Urbina.

I offered to show him battlefield positions. We went to see the batteries and when we advanced further Gonzalitos met us and guided us by way of the best protected roads. In the ruins of the La Plata mine we examined the large yards in preparation of advancing the batteries through them during the night. I ordered Espinosa de los Monteros to bring Major Jurado so I could show him the positions that his three batteries must take that night, and I showed Saavedra the position for one of his near the village next to the mine in front of La Bufa. Gonzalitos pointed out to me another very good position from which we could fire on La Bufa as well as the hill next to it; and I commissioned him to notify Saavedra and order him to take that position during the night.

On the way back I took General Villa to the position of Quiroz. From there I showed him the entire battlefield. He told me: "You and Urbina will enter through there, in front of the batteries; I will come from the right flank, and also attack the hill of Loreto." Urbina recommended that the battery of Quiroz fire on a hill that flanked the troops of General Villa's, which would be attacking Loreto.

As I was leaving, General Villa ordered me together with the Zaragoza brigade to relieve the part of Morelos that would support the artillery.

We ordered the Zaragoza brigade to advance in broken formation. There was one exposed area and there we ordered the troops to pass in small groups and at a gallop. In the creek bed behind our position that had the artillery the troop of the brigade dismounted and formed on foot.

Madero, Major Ángeles, Cervantes, Espinosa de los Monteros and I advanced to show the officer in charge the positions that his troop must relieve.

The night was damp, cloudy and very dark. The only light was from the spotlight atop La Bufa that turned continuously, stopping occasionally to illuminate terrain it vainly wanted to explore.

In spite of the fact that I had been over the area various times in the daylight, tonight I had difficulty. Several times I stepped into pools that had formed from the heavy rainfall. Fortunately. we met a boy from our vanguard that guided us.

Our return was difficult. Sometimes the limited light from the spotlight seemed to follow us. At last we found troops from the Zaragoza Brigade on foot and they pointed out where our horses were. We mounted and left for Vetagrande under a light rain by the shortest road, not the one we used before because at that time we had needed go out of formation.

Only our guide was able to follow the road, the rest of us walked carefully in his footsteps, trusting and silent. It was a procession of ghosts, stretching alongside an enemy who dreamed nightmares lying there beneath that spotlight that was nothing but a symptom of fear; serving no purpose other than to make one believe that it was accomplishing something.

We dined gaily in the company of don Angel Caso and two doctors from the medical service of the Zaragoza Brigade. The former asked me where the battle would be fought the following day.

We slept well.

June 23, 1914

We woke late, I shaved, bathed and changed my under clothing; we breakfasted and mounted our horses; I was riding my Curely, brilliant and muscular.

An aide of Colonel Gonzalitos came asking written instructions; I gave them and repeated them verbally when Gonzalitos and I met later.

We went to see General Ceniceros to explain his mission in the combat. He and Gonzalitos were to take the hill of black land next to La Bufa, under cover of fire from the batteries of Saavedra. Raúl Madero would take the hill of red soil (that of Loreto), under the cover of the batteries of Jurado at the same time that the troops with General Villa would be attacking from the right.

We left our horses protected from bullets and advanced on foot to the ruins of the La Plata mine.

Overnight, our artillery had disappeared from their original locations and taken other positions much closer to the enemy but hidden from their sight. Three batteries (of Jurado's group) were located inside the large corrals of the La Plata mine. One of Saavedra's was next to the ruins on the plain, but behind the crest of a minute hill in front of La Bufa; another on the extreme left, also in front of La Bufa but well protected behind a crest; a third battery of the Saavedra group remained on the high hill of Vetagrande

The enemy must have been surprised at the disappearance of our batteries that had been silent for two days in spite of rifle bullets whistling by them like speedy mosquitoes.

Inside the large corrals we found Raúl Madero; "all is ready, my General, he said. "But it is not quite 9:00 o clock. At 10:00 o' clock we must begin the battle."

Engineer Enrique Valle came running and told me, "I come to put myself at your orders for whatever I can do to serve. Do you understand me?"

An officer from General Aguirre Benavides told me that the Robles Brigade was awaiting orders from someone. "It would be helpful," I answered, "to use you as reserve." But later I decided his troops would be more useful attacking the hill of the black earth, and I invited him to join General Ceniceros and Colonel Gonzalitos.

I ordered all the *jefes* to present themselves and I reiterated orders for the attacks. In only twenty more minutes everything had to be in place, ready to fire at precisely10:00 o'clock.

In the distance, from the direction of *Hacienda Nueva,* we heard the first gun shot. There came General Villa! The battle had begun!

The twenty-four canons closest to us, positioned between Vetagrande and Zacatecas roared, their projectiles ripping the air with shrieks of death and exploded, some on the hill of black soil, others on Loreto. The very depths of the mountains next to us seemed to be ripped a thousand times by the echo. And the infantry troops advanced over the emerald mantle that covered the slope.

On the side of San Antonio, there by the high plateau and by the Villa de Guadalupe, canons and rifles and thousands of whistling projectiles thundered. Echoes from the mountains prolonged the sound of detonations, like yards of cloth being ripped on their flanks.

That epic concert intensified as additional canons thundered from Zacatecas, El Grillo, La Bufa, the hill of Clérigos, and all the federal positions.

Enemy shells began to explode in our direction; but they were very high and very long.

Someone said that they believed we were too far away, behind the protective walls; another assured us that the federals were firing on our cavalry that had entered the action from the right. Other shells fell behind us, perhaps shot over the closest battery of Saavedra.

Another came running to inform us that a battery to the right of Jurado was being hit by enemy artillery; another said that two mules had been killed as well as one grenade thrower; a third had taken down the main piece of the nearest battery, that of Saavedra.

"Come and see, my General, through here, through this space, see how almost all the blows fall behind the battery. The first piece is now unmanned, and the others are immobile behind the armor." The shells of the enemy were zooming and exploding in the air launching their sheaf of shrapnel or rebounding with a dry blow that exploded later sending their shrapnel forward into the earth or the rocks on the ground, a tragic and terrorizing hurricane.

I returned to my original observation point where I could not see the effect of the batteries that fired against the hill of black soil but where I could perceive the effect of the battery that battered the red hill, the hill of Loreto.

Perhaps there where the red soil had been removed our shells would also blow their tragic hurricane; but from our viewpoint we just seemed to be tickling the enemy. After a few minutes it seemed our shells were falling on abandoned parapets and trenches because the little black dots that moved around at first on the red soil had now disappeared.

Our soldiers were shouting with joy!

"Look at our men! How close they are to the enemy. See, ours is the most forward flag!

"Look! Look! Look what is happening! See how they are running away!"

The canons lengthened their shots, and our infantry began a furious attack. The tri-color flag was raised in the position of conquest. It was only twenty-five minutes after ten in the morning.

A short time later, the flank of access to the hill of Loreto was populated with our infantry that climbed slowly and painfully; the horses were also arriving slowly. Later all could be seen in formation and protected.

The time had come to change our position. I asked Major Cervantes to order our horses brought so we could go survey Loreto to decide the best route to take and the next placement of Jurado's group of canons.

Captain Durón was shelling effectively in the intermediate position between Loreto and El Grillo. I authorized him to continue.

As I galloped with my staff toward Loreto, we met General Villa and his retinue; He came on his powerful red, saying that he needed artillery sited in Loreto. "It's on the way my general," I replied. We proceeded along the road to Loreto.

Did the enemy realize that General Villa would be travelling in a group such as ours? Perhaps; at least they guessed that this joint meeting of two groups of staff officers was important because the path of their firing followed us. The *Jefe* took charge and we obeyed. Who fell on the road? We hoped it was not General Villa. Bullets whistled by encrusting the ground with a dry thud.

The horse of Major Barzán was injured on one hoof and his assistant was injured on his arm…our only causalities.

In Loreto the rain of shells was heavy. Where did they come from? Who knew? But I did not try to fire on my mysterious enemy. All our attention was focused on helping the infantry attack of General Servín who was climbing up the sides of the hill La Sierpe and was at the point of being thrown back.

All our troops from Loreto were firing against the summit of La Sierpe without helping Servín it seemed. General Villa established a machine gun in an angle of a house and also opened fire on the summit of La Sierpe, but that did not facilitate the advance of Servín either.

And the artillery did not arrive; the minutes seemed like hours!

At last a canon came and then others from the command of Durón. The first canon blast sounded happily in our ears and probably very disagreeably in the ears of the defenders of La Sierpe. That first shot was on target and boosted the morale of our troops coming from Loreto, and after fifteen minutes the enemy began to evacuate their position; Our tricolor fluttered on the summit and our soldiers began shouting frenetic, enthusiastic hurrahs. The entire infantry of Servín scrambled up the pine-covered sides of La Sierpe to that much-desired summit.

And because this summit dominates El Grillo, taking it was the second step in conquering the strongest position of the enemy.

The canons that battered Sierpe could not be used from the same position to attack El Grillo: I had to place them to the front of the houses, in a small patio that had a circular wall facing the enemy with openings the canons could use. But that side of the houses was blasted by a hurricane of death. Bullets from rifles whistled rapidly and the shells exploded thunderously. Very few bodies remained erect; few heads remained high.

I gave the order to Captain Durón to bring artillery and place them in battery mode in front of the houses, where the machinegun used to be, and a little later I sent the remaining pieces to the left.

It was on that side, behind the houses that I found a disorderly mound of soldiers, horses, carriages, artillery with shells that were unfired, but without operators or officers.

It was difficult to make operators and officers reappear and move the canons to the patio I mentioned. They had to cross a narrow road that was very visible to the enemy and a perfect distance for their artillery. It was necessary to use my revolver and muster the fiercest energy.

The same persuasion that moved the artillery also moved the straggling infantry. Men advanced with backs bent in an effort to be protected by the circular wall. From there we pushed them toward the enemy showing them as an example the rest of the infantry that was battling the enemy a thousand meters further ahead. The forced charge by our straggling infantry was very interesting. It seemed that a formidable wind blew in their face and made them fall back when they were ordered to advance. Bless the soldiers of the village, obliged by duty to be heroes they advanced although their souls trembled, and their knees weakened!

One battery remained in that patio, a battery that kept firing at El Grillo in spite of receiving fire not only from that artillery but also from above, from La Bufa.

If they drove us back from Loreto, if they drove back the artillery, it would not be possible for our infantry to continue on El Grillo: it was necessary to rush boldly, in spite of the violent fire of the enemy that was almost entirely concentrated on Loreto. The artillery, a moment earlier terrorized, was newly fired up and courageous. Now they were working heroically in the middle of a rain of lead and steel.

General Villa, stood on a pile of stones to follow the work of the artillerymen attentively as well as the slow and painful progress of the infantry and the feverish activity of the enemy, who could feel their coming defeat in the rough advance of the Division del Norte, though maybe not the great sacrifice in the great final graveyard that loomed. Suddenly there was a huge explosion. Three meters from us there was a cloud of smoke and dust. There were shouts of terror. We thought an enemy bomb had hit point blank on the spot next to us and had killed all the operators.

When the smoke and dust had dissipated we saw various dead, one with two hands blown off, blood congealing on bones of his forearms, his head gone and belly destroyed and clothing blackened, he lay immobile, as if he had been dead for hours. Another indelible impression was that of a wounded man who had the face of a ghost and a thread of blood pouring from half open lips that were trembling in pain.

It had not been an enemy bomb; but a one of our own shells that exploded as the crew prepared to fire it. We could not allow our artillerymen to reflect on the danger of handling grenades. It was necessary to distract them by whatever means.

"Nothing happened," I shouted at them, "Don't stop! Some must die, and some must live. To live we must kill the enemy. Fire without ceasing!"

The fire continued stronger than before. General Villa stepped back a few steps and lay down on a heap of sand. He said to me sadly, "You don't know what pain the death of one of my boys causes me. When the enemy kills them, it happens; but death from our own weapons causes me pain".

"What shall we do," he continued, "so that our infantry can continue to advance? They seem to me a bit broken" .

"They are very tired", I answered, "and one single advance is not going to dislodge the enemy from all their positions. Would you like Cervantes order the infantry to advance?"

Cervantes left us, happy to be used on this mission.

We could see him afar, with his hat tilted to one side, galloping rhythmically on his sorrel horse.

General Raúl Madero said that his troops were exhausted and he requested fresh troops to launch the attack on El Grillo.

My assistant, Baca brought food that we shared with General Villa and the other officers there. We ate contentedly sitting inside a large house with a roof that looked like a sieve because of holes made by our shells. I had never seen that much destruction with so much pleasure.

To aide our digestion Cervantes and I went for a walk, we came across a severely wounded horse that moved us with pity. We put him out of his pain. The detonations of our pistols seemed faint to our deafened ears.

The noise of the battle became more perceptible as we drew closer and we returned with rekindled passion.

I knew almost from the beginning of the attack that my battery had to leave the position that was attacking La Bufa and move to continue the attack on El Grillo.

Where was Gonzalitos? What was he doing? Had he eaten? Was he wounded?

I decided we would move to the other side of the battlefield and left a message for General Villa explaining my departure.

I sent an order to Captain Quiroz to leave the high hill at Vetegrande and move to El Grillo where he would receive further orders. I felt certain that in the time it took Quiroz to move, El Grillo would be in our power.

We were enjoying a gallop on our horses, when Gonzalitos appeared limping. He had dislocated his foot. "Yes sir, I have eaten," he told me with a smile.

All was going well on that side; the slope of the black soil hill was taken earlier and now those soldiers were fighting with those defending La Bufa.

I gave the command for one of the batteries of Saavedra to advance to the slope that was on the backside of the black soil. From that place we had an admirable view of Zacatecas, La Bufa and the road from Zacatecas to Guadalupe. On the other side of

Zacatecas, between La Bufa and El Grillo, were troops, probably those of Herrera, Chao and Ortega. They had taken over a white house with a large corral adjacent to it.

Near our position there were some straggling infantrymen, those who always found some excuse to stay behind.

The battery of Saavedra settled into the new position and opened fire on La Bufa.

Now the fight took on the aspect of the complete victory to come. The resistance from La Bufa and El Grillo was weakening. I could see it was just a question of time until the idea of defeat germinated in the mind of the enemy.

Yellow smoke soon arose from the city as if it were mixed with dust. Perhaps it was a fire, perhaps an explosion. We checked our watches: it was 5:50 in the afternoon.

Our troops were encircling the enemy and tightening the noose. What was the enemy going to do? Where did they intend to retreat?

Engineer Valle, Major Cervantes, my brother[108] and I saw many troops on the road from Zacatecas to Guadalupe. It pleased us to be able see them so distinctly.

Meanwhile the enemy could be seen; soldiers in groups and others trying to get into formation. Then we noticed a thin line of infantry that preceded the cavalry, formed into a dense column. What did they intend? Perhaps they were going to retreat? But in that formation!

We saw them advance toward Guadalupe, and then retreat in disorder. They could not discern our troops who were driving them back.

Soon the enemy moved toward Jerez, and then retreated. They were intending to go through Vetagrande, on the side where we had sent the stragglers to hunt them.

"Don't worry", I told them, "they are not going to fight, they are going to hide. You have nothing to do but exterminate them. The enemy will be turned back."

Finally, they seemed to be making one final desperate retreat in the direction they had originally chosen, the road toward Guadalupe. And they were in almost complete disarray. We did not see their fall, but we could imagine it. I confess without shame, that if I saw them annihilated it would have given me the greatest delight; because I saw it from the point of view of an artist, the success of a completed work, a finished masterpiece. And I sent to General Villa this message: "We have won, my General"! And effectively the battle was over even though there were still many shots still to be fired.

In the distance to the South, the battlefront of generals Herrera, Chao, and Ortega; the place where the white house and large corral were located, the flash of priming shots from the resplendent canons looked like tiny shards of mirrored glass.

Little by little the black dots began to descend from El Grillo running toward the City.

Below us at the edge of the road to Vetagrande we saw a dam with clean blue water next to some peaceful houses. We walked down to see it, no longer concerned about the battle.

As we were rejoicing about the batteries on our left, we could hear the canon blasts better from those to our right, they were firing against El Grillo; from whose crest the federal troops were retreating slowly and apparently tranquilly.

A great quiet reigned in the abandoned houses next to the dam, disturbed only by the braying of a couple of donkeys. Once in a while, a bullet would zoom by, lost no doubt.

Major Cervantes, at the side of Engineer Valle and of Major Ángeles, stretched out on their bellies on the ground, supported behind by their toes and in front by their elbows with their *sombreros,* half off their heads so that they could see the details of combat in the camp opposite on La Bufa, between the houses of picturesque Zacatecas. Or further away, the white house next to the corral, where in plain view they could see some silhouettes of horsemen and the colorful group of Carrillo's batteries.

Margarito Orozco, the courageous and maimed enthusiast, galloped up on his spirited horse. "Buenas tardes, my general, it seems we are going to leave soon"

I dismounted and we walked around the pond and sat on the wall of the dam to talk of our ideals of the happiness of the whole world. I was enchanted by the great and good soul of my friend.

One of our soldiers came from Zacatecas, dying of thirst; he drank by lifting water to his mouth in his hand. The afternoon breeze brought the stench of a dead horse lying a few steps away

I returned to join my group of assistants and saw the top of Grillo filled with our troops who came down from right to left above Zacatecas and I also we saw that our troops had begun to enter La Bufa, from the left.

Now, I thought, we lack only the final phase, the disagreeable part, our entrance into the conquered city bringing death to the straggling enemies who are going to leave this world filled with terror.

Cervantes and Valle wanted to see this phase of the battle: I commissioned them to go into Zacatecas right away to look for lodging for troops and officers. Meanwhile, I went to Vetegrande to arrange for moving the hospital and kitchens.

Captain Espinosa de la Monteros was commissioned to carry the order for the batteries to move to Zacatecas and stay wherever Major Cervantes indicated, an order that was received with happy hurrahs.

It was 6:45 in the afternoon; the temperature was delicious; the sun of this glorious day of June 23rd died peacefully.

I returned with my brother and my aide. We could now walk tranquilly through that terrain that had been in enemy hands for so long and a few hours ago had been furiously contested. The main street of Zacatecas was visible through an entry raked by enemy shells.

"Boys, you can now go to Zacatecas: the city is ours," I told soldiers that we were meeting on the road.

Doctor Wichman vacillated at first and followed us at a great distance; but at last decided to enter Zacatecas that same evening.

In Vetagrande they received the news of the triumph with great gusto.

Stretched out peacefully on my field cot I revisited the phases of the classic battle; a miracle given the untrained revolutionary troops who had been organized and instructed even as they were assembling.

I reviewed the principle attack made on the lines La Bufa, El Grillo the front by the troops of Ceniceros, Aguirre Benavides, Gonzalitos and Raúl Madero, supported by the artillery and the flanking troops of Trinidad and Jose Rodriguez, of don Rosalio

Hernandez, Almanza and the entire infantry: all together ten thousand men.

When the principle defense was defeated, and the garrison could no longer continue to resist because La Bufa and El Grillo dominated the city, they tried to escape via the southern route or by the East. However, exit to the South was impractical because the lines of communication were to the East by way of Guadalupe toward Aguascalientes. Three-thousand of our men were enough to prevent the retreat by that route. In contrast, in Guadalupe a strong reserve was necessary, seven thousand men centered in Guadalupe plus troops on the flanks, obstructed the retreat through Jerez and Vetagrande. It was there we gave the final blow to the enemy already demoralized by the main attack and ready to abandon the city.

And in the development of the action: what adjustments and what harmony in the collaboration between the infantry and the artillery! The artillery worked in unison with the exclusive object of hitting and neutralizing the enemy in the positions our infantry wanted to conquer; only one battery was used against an opposing battery; and the infantry moved resolutely on the position after the neutralization had been accomplished. What satisfaction to have reached this cooperation of arms so recently initiated in San Pedro de Las Colonias with Madero and Aguirre Benavides, so much perfection after the confusion of Torreón, won by force, tenacity and courage! And I had to appreciate how the whole world needed this kind of harmony and cooperation.

I reviewed the battle condensed into one attack using two branches of our army in a harmonious concert: the retreat to the South blocked, and the reserve to the East able to give the *coupe de gras* to the enemy in disarray.

And over that theoretic concept that summed up a great battle plan, I collected episodes that impressed me the most: the precision of the battle's phases; the impetuosity of the attack; the hurricane of steel and lead; the explosions of armaments multiplied to infinity by echoes that simulated a cataclysm; the heroic force of the weak souls that moved hunched over against the tempest of death; the sudden and tragic deaths following the explosion of the shells; the wounded full of fear and immense horror that saw the implacable approach of death; the heroics of the wounded like Rodolfo Fierro spouting blood, forgetful of his own person yet able to participate effectively in combat; or the wounded that were unable to continue the fight who sadly left the battle like the intrepid Trinidad Rodríguez, who was surprised by death while life was telling him lovingly, "Don't go, it is not time yet". So many things, many beautiful things; and finally, in the afternoon, serenity with the full certainty of victory that came with a loving smile to caress the face of Francisco Villa the brave and glorious soldier of the people.

It was a beautiful sight. The mathematical precision of artillery produced the precise result in a precise way. That was beautiful. Under the enchantment of the classic masterpiece of that happy day, I sank placidly into a restorative dream without apprehensions.

June 24, 1914

On the following morning we entered Zacatecas visiting the battlefield on the side near La Bufa: squadrons of vultures had been hard at work on the enemy. There were few dead there; but almost all were atrociously wounded, and their positions revealed a painful agony.

Courtesy of the National Historical Archive of Zacatecas

Looking like looters, we scavenged for useful equipment and munitions. We stationed vigilantes to guard the things we wanted and sent troops to retrieve them. Inside the city there were many more dead, invariably with wounds to the head. The accumulation of our soldiers made all parts of the streets impassable. Ruins of a building, the Department of Armaments, filled the cross streets. They said that in the city entire families had perished in the destruction of that building, blown up by the federal troops for what reason I don't know.

There were so many troops in Zacatecas that Cervantes could not find a place to billet the artillery and he decided to look in the direction of Aguascalientes, in Guadalupe or further toward the lagoon of Pedernalillo, whose mirrored surface we had seen the first time we climbed the high hill of Vetagrande.

Oh! The road from Zacatecas to Guadalupe: an infinite tenderness oppressed by heart. What caused me such joy the evening before because it indicated an unequivocal triumph now moved me deeply.

Both sides of the road were filled with cadavers, to the extent that it was impossible for carriages to pass on the seven kilometers of road between Zacatecas and Guadalupe and the regions nearby, both sides of the road were filled with cadavers, to the extent that it was impossible for carriages to pass. The bodies lying there amounted to at least eighty percent of those federals killed.

Dead horses had neither saddles nor bridles and the soldiers had neither weapons, nor shoes. Many did not even have clothing.

The quality of the underclothing revealed that many of the dead had been officers.

Thanks to the cold temperatures of Zacatecas, the cadavers did not even smell, and it was possible to observe them without repugnance.

All the horses were inflated with gases, with their legs rigid and separated. Looters had already been at the soldiers removing shoes, and exterior clothing. There was an infinity of facial expressions; those who died peacefully only seemed to be sleeping, but some remained in attitudes of desperation with grimaces of pain and terror.

And I thought, "the major part of those deaths were probably enemies of Huerta and could have been friends of ours. I knew that some of them were my friends and only inertia of the herd kept them on the side of injustice!"

In Guadalupe (as in Zacatecas) the residents were terrified. Would their properties be respected? "It is alright," said one, "to allow the soldiers whatever they wanted: but respect my life and that of my wife and children".

One woman had a premature birth and had died of fright.

All asked safe conduct, and all disputed the honor of inviting the main officers to dinner, so that they would give them guarantees.

The war, for us the officers, was full of charms that produced infinite sadness and shame; but everyone must see it as part of his job. What for some is calamity, for others is a great art.

I stayed in the mine of La Fe with my general staff; the troop stayed in Guadalupe.

We were very grateful for the comfortable hospitality that the Noble family gave us.

June 25, 1914

The terrible defeat suffered by Huerta's army at Zacatecas broke the morale of the enemy and began the retreat of Huerta's generals both east to San Luis and west Guadalajara.

It would be possible for the Division del Norte to march triumphantly into the capital city, Mexico D.F

Mounted on my Turena who leaped gracefully over walls and wide ditches, I went to see General Villa and requested four brigades of cavalry to take Aguascalientes. "I am going to give you seven, my general." And he gave orders to the *jefes* of those seven; and I gave mine the order to leave the following day. Eagerly I rubbed my hands together; I was certain that on Sunday we would enter Aguascalientes.

But fate had other plans.

An unexpected order arrived from General Villa that we should return to Torreon. Our commander had been sleepless thinking of the situation of the Division del Norte.

The glorious victory in Zacatecas increased Carranza's fury. Jealousy of Villa and his popularity with the people, made Carranza desperate to prevent Villa from entering Mexico City as the conquering hero. Instead of congratulations on an amazing victory Carranza became openly hostile toward the Division del Norte and ordered Villa's supply of coal be cut. Without coal Villa could not move his trains. Because of two great battles (Torreon and Zacatecas) we had no munitions; we were not allowed to bring munitions through Ciudad Juarez; neither would our friends allow us to go to Tampico for arms, nor would Carranza allow us to get coal from Monclova.

General Villa did not want to compromise his line of supply with the border: his locomotives were out of coal. Our return to the North became indispensable.

Carranza sent Licenciado Miguel Alessio Robles, from the army of the Northeast to initiate talks with us. He informed us that their attitude was entirely harmonious and if we disobeyed the order that General Villa give up the command of the Division of the North, it would bring due consequences very harmful to the cause and to the nation that we were obliged to avoid. He demanded that we make no further plans for a rapid march to México City and that we invite the Army of the Northeast to go San Luis Potosí.

The response to Licenciado Alessio Robles was to decline the invitation.

July 8, 1914.

It was sad and at the same time comfortable to ride on our trains over the fields of the State of Chihuahua!

A rapid parade of posts and bushes is passing by the square of the window across from which I write these notes on my knees.

FELÍPE ÁNGELES, JUNE 1914

This was the inglorious ending of the Battle of Zacatecas. The Division del Norte was prevented in making a direct march to Mexico City. However, the Battle of Zacatecas so devastated the power of the federal army that Victoriano Huerta left the country a few weeks later. The parties of the revolution were successful in unseating the usurper, but they failed to agree on how to govern the nation. A political battle would soon ensue between the Constitutionalists (Carranza and Obregon) and the Conventionists (Villa, Maytorena, and Ángeles). Civil war became inevitable.

The End

APPENDIX A
TREATY OF JUAREZ

The most significant point of the treaty signed on May 21, 1911 was that President Porfirio Diaz, and his vice president, Ramon Corral, resign and that Francisco Leon de la Barra, acting as Interim President, would organize free elections as soon as possible.

The treaty also provided amnesty for all revolutionaries and gave the option for some of them to apply for membership in a rural army or guard called *rurales.* The Revolutionary forces were demobilized immediately, and federal forces were the only army in Mexico. Madero ordered that to appease the army which opposed any compromise with him.

Madero claimed the right to name fourteen provisional state governors and to approve de la Barra's cabinet.

Policemen and judges, as well as state legislators, that had been appointed or elected under Diaz were to retain their positions, and pensions were to be established for relatives of soldiers who died fighting for the rebels.

The treaty was signed on May 21. Diaz resigned on May 25. Francisco de la Barra became Interim President.

Elections were held five months later on October 15 and Francisco I. Madero took office on November 6, 1911.

Plan De Alaya

November 25,1911.

Liberating Plan of the sons of the State of Morelos, affiliated with the Insurgent Army which defends the fulfillment of the Plan od San Luis, with the reforms which it has believed proper to add in benefit of the Mexican Fatherland.

We who undersign, constituted in a revolutionary junta to sustain and carry out the promises which the revolution of November 20, 1910 just past, made to the country, declare solemnly before the face of the civilized world which judges us and before the nation to which we belong and which we all love, propositions which we have formulated to end the tyranny which oppresses us and redeem the fatherland from the dictatorships which are impose on us, which (propositions) are determined in the following plan:

1. Taking into consideration that the Mexican people led by Don Francisco I Madero we to shed their blood to reconquer liberties and recover their rights which have been trampled on, and not for a man to take possession of power, violating the sacred principles which he took an oath to defend under the slogan "Effective Suffrage and No Reelection," outraging thus the faith, the cause, the justice, and the liberties of the people: taking into consideration that that man to whom we refer is Don Francisco I. Madero, the same who initiated the above-cited revolution, who imposed his will and influence a governing norm on the Provisional Government of the ex-President of the Republic Attorney Francisco L. de

Barra, causing with this deed repeated shedding of blood and multiplicate misfortunes for the fatherland in a manner deceitful and ridiculous, having no intentions other than satisfying his personal ambitions, his boundless instincts as a tyrant, and his profound disrespect for the fulfillment of the preexisting laws emanating from the immortal code of '57, written with the revolutionary blood of Ayutla;

Taking into account that the so-called Chief of the Liberating Revolution of Mexico, Don Francisco I. Madero, through lack of honesty and the highest weakness, did not carry to a happy end the revolution which gloriously he initiated with the help of God and the people, since he left standing most of the governing powers and corrupted elements of oppression of the dictatorial government of Porfirio Diaz, which are not nor can in any way be the representation of National Sovereignty, and which, for being most bitter adversaries of ours and of the principles which even now we defend, are provoking the discomfort of the country and opening new wounds in the bosom of the fatherland, to give it its own blood to drink, taking also into account that the aforementioned Sr. Francisco I. Madero, President of the Republic, tries to avoid the fulfillment of the promises which he made to the Nation in the Plan of San Luis Potosi, restricting the above-cited promises to the agreements of Ciudad Juarez, by means of false promises and numerous intrigues against the Nation nullifying, pursuing, jailing, or killing revolutionary elements who helped him to occupy the high post of President of the Republic;

Taking into consideration that the so-often-repeated Francisco I. Madero has tried with the brute force of bayonets to shut up and to drown in blood the pueblos who ask, solicit, or demand from him the fulfillment of the promises of the revolution, calling them bandits and rebels, condemning them to a war of extermination without conceding or granting a single one of the guarantees which reason, justice and the law prescribe; taking equally into consideration that the President of the Republic Francisco I Madero has made of Effective Suffrage a bloody trick on people, already against the will of the same people imposing Attorney Jose M. Pino Suarez in the Vice-Presidency of the Republic, or imposing as Governors of the States men designated by him, like the so-called General Ambrosio Figueroa, scourge and tyrant of the people of Morelos or entering into scandalous cooperation with the cientifico party, feudal landlords, and oppressive bosses, enemies of the revolution proclaimed by him, so as to forge new chains and follow the pattern of a new dictatorship more shameful and more terrible than that of Porfirio Diaz, for it has been clear and patent that he has outraged the sovereignty of the States, trampling on the laws without any respect for lives or interests, as has happened in the State of Morelos, and others, leading them to the most horrendous anarchy which contemporary history registers.

For these considerations we declare the aforementioned Francisco I Madero inept at realizing the promises of the revolution of which he was the author, because he has betrayed the principles with which he tricked the will of the people and was able to get into power: incapable of governing, because he has no respect for the law and justice of the pueblos, and a traitor to the fatherland because he is humiliating in blood and fire Mexicans who want liberties, so as to please the cientificos, landlords, and bosses who enslave us, and from today on we begin to continue the revolution begun by him, until we achieve the overthrow of the dictatorial powers which exist.

2. Recognition is withdrawn from Sr. Francisco I. Madero as Chief of the Revolution is withdrawn from Sr. Francisco I. Madero as Chief of the Revolution and a President of the Republic, for the reasons which before

were expressed, it being attempted to overthrow this official.

3. Recognized as Chief of the Liberating Revolution is the illustrious General Pascual Orozco, the second of the Leader Don Francisco I. Madero, and in case he does not accept his delicate post, recognition as Chief of the Revolution will go to General Don Emiliano Zapata.

4. The Revolutionary Junta of the State of Morelos manifests to the Nation under formal oath: that it makes its own plan of San Luis Potosi, with the additions which are expressed below in benefit of the oppressed pueblos, and it will make itself the defender of the principles it defends until victory or death.

5. The Revolution Junta of the State of Morelos will admit no transactions or compromises until it achieves the overthrow of the dictatorial elements of Porfirio Diaz and Francisco I. Madero, for the nation is tired of false men and traitors who make promises like liberators and who on arriving in power forget them and constitute themselves as tyrants.

6. As an additional part of the plan we invoke, we give notice: that (regarding) the fields, timber, and water which the landlords, cientificos, or bosses have the titles corresponding to those properties will immediately enter into possession of that real estate of which they have been despoiled by the bad faith of our oppressors, maintaining at any cost with arms in hand the mentioned possession; and the usurpers who consider themselves with a right to them (those properties) will deduce it before the special tribunals which will be established on the triumph of the revolution.

7. In virtue of the fact that the immense majority of Mexican pueblos and citizens are owners of no more than the land they walk on, suffering the horrors of poverty without being able to improve their social condition in any way or to dedicate themselves to industry or Agriculture, because land, timber, and water are monopolized in a few hands, for this cause there will be expropriated the third part of those monopolies from the powerful proprietors of them, with prior indemnization, in order that the pueblos and citizens of Mexico why obtain ejidos, colonies, and foundations for pueblos, or fields for sowing or laboring, and the Mexican' lack of prosperity and wellbeing may improve in all and for all.

8. (Regarding) The Landlords, cientificos, or bosses who oppose the present plan directly or indirectly, their goods will be nationalized and the two thirds parts which (otherwise would) belong to them will go for indemnizations of war, pensions for widows and orphans of the victims who succumb in the struggle for the present plan.

9. In order to execute the procedures regarding the properties aforementioned, the laws of disamortization and nationalization will be applied as they fit, for serving us as norm and example can be those laws put in force by the immortal Juarez on ecclesiastical properties, which punished the despots and conservatives who in every time have tried to impose on us the ignominious yoke of oppression and backwardness.

10. The insurgent military chiefs of the Republic who rose up with arms in hand at the voice of Don Francisco I. Madero to defend the plan of San Luis Potosi, and to oppose with armed force the present plan, will be judged traitors to the cause which they defended and to the

fatherland, since at present many of them, to humor tyrants, for a fistful of coins, or for bribes or connivance, are shedding the blood of their brothers who claim the fulfillment of promises which Don Francisco I. Madero made to the nation.

11. The expenses of war will be taken in conformity with Article II of the Plan of San Luis Potosi, and all procedures employed in the revolution we undertake will be in conformity with the same instructions which the said plan determines.

12. Once triumphant the revolution which we carry into the path of reality, a Junta of the principal revolutionary chiefs from the different States will name or designate an interim president of the Republic, who will convoke elections for the organization of federal powers.

13. The principal revolutionary chiefs of each State will designate in Junta the Governor of the State to which they belong, and this appointed official will convoke elections for the due organization of the public powers, the object being to avoid compulsory appointments which work the misfortune of the pueblos, like the so-well-known appointment of Ambrosio Figueroa in the State of Morelos and others who drive us to the precipice of bloody conflicts, sustained by the caprice of the dictator Madero and the circle of cientificos and landlords who have influenced him.

14. If President Madero and other dictatorial elements of the present and former regime want to avoid the immense misfortunes which afflict the fatherland, and (if they) possess true sentiments of love for it, let them make immediate renunciation of the posts they occupy and with that they will something staunch the grave wounds

which they have opened in the bosom of the fatherland, since if they do not do so, on their heads will fall the blood and the anathema of our brothers.

15. Mexicans: consider that the cunning and bad faith of one man is shedding blood in a scandalous manner, because he is incapable of governing; consider that his system of government is choking the fatherland and trampling with the brute force of bayonets on our institutions; and thus, as we raised up our weapons to elevate him to power, we again raise them up against him for defaulting on his promises to the Mexican people and for having betrayed the revolution initiated by him we are not personalists; we are partisans of principles and not of men!

Mexican People, support this plan with arms in hand and you will make the prosperity and well-being of the fatherland.

Ayala, November 25, 1911
Liberty, Justice, and Law

Signed, *General in Chief Emiliano Zapata; Generals Eufemio Zapata, Francisco Mendoza, Jesús Morales, Jesús Navarro, Otilio E. Montaño José Trinidad Ruiz, Proculo Capistrån; Colonés Felípe Vaquero, Cesáreo Burgos, Quintín González, Pedro Salazar, Simón Rojas, Emigdio Marmolejo, José Campos, Pioquinto Galis, Felípe Tijera, Rafael Sánchez, José Pérez, Santiago Aguilar, Margarito Martínez, Feliciano Domínguez, Manuel Vergara, Cruz Salazar, Lauro Sánchez, Amador Salazar, Lorenzo Vázquez, Catarino Perdomo, Jesús Sánchez, Domingo Romero, Zacarías Torres, Bonifacio García, Daniel Andrade, Ponciano Domínguez, Jesús Capistran; Captains Daniel Mantilla, José M. Carrillo, Francisco Alarcón, Severiano Gutiérrez; and more signatures follow. (this is a true copy taken from the original. Camp in the Mountains of Puebla, December 11, 1911. Signed, General in Chief, Emiliano Zapata.*[109]

APPENDIX C
Plan Of Guadalupe

Manifesto to the Nation

Considering that General Victoriano the defense of the institutions and legality of his government, when siding with the enemies who rebelled against that same government, to restore the latest dictatorship, committed the crime of treason to scale in power, arresting the president and vice-president, as well as their ministers, demanding of them by violent means to renounce their posts, which is verified by the messages that the same General Huerta sent to the to the Governors of the States communicating to them that he had taken prisoner the Supreme Magistrates of the nation and their cabinet. Considering that the Legislative and Judicial Powers in spite of the laws and constitutional rules have recognized and protected General Victoriano Huerta and his illegal and unpatriotic procedures, and considering, finally, that some Governemnts of the States of the Union have recognized the illegitimate Government imposed by that part of the Army that carried out the treason, headed by the same general Huerta, in spite of having violated the sovereignty of those states, whose Governors should have been the first to not recognize him, the following subscribers, Chief and Officers commanding the Constitutional forces, have agreed and will sustain with arms the following:

PLAN

I.   General Victoriano Huerta is not recognized as President of the Republic   .

2. The Legislative and Judicial Powers of the Federation are also not recognized.
3. The Governments of the States that still recognize the Federal Powers that form the present administration, are also not recognized thirty days after the publication of this Plan.
4. For the Organization of the Army entrusted with fulfilling our intentions, we name as First Chief of the Army that will be denominated "Constitutionalist", the citizen Venustiano Carranza Governor of the State of Coahuila.
5. When the Constitutionalist Army occupies Mexico City, the citizen Venustiano Carranza, First Chief of the Army, will be in interim charge of the Executive Power, or whoever would have substituted him in command.
6. The interim president of the republic will call for general elections as soon as peace has been consolidated, handing over power to the citizen who is elected.
7. The citizen acting as First Chief of the Constitutionalist Army in the states whose governments have recognized that of Huerta, will assume command as provisional governor and will call for local elections, after having taken possession of their posts the citizens having been elected to carry out the powers of the federation, as called for by the previous rule.

***

This document was the immediate answer of the Constitutionalist forces against the military coup d'état against the regime of Francisco I. Madero. Victoriano Huerta announced his assumption of power on February 18, 1913 and had been in power only 36 days when those who opposed his illegal act announced their official resistance.

APPENDIX D
The Lerdo Law

The Lerdo Law was authored by Miguel Lerdo de Tejada, Finance Minister of Mexico in 1856. The law was enacted by President Ignacio Comonfort on June 25, 1856. The law was intended to develop a middle-class in rural Mexico, stimulate real estate sales, and raise funds for the federal treasury by means of a 5% tax on each sale. The law prohibited ecclesiastical and civil corporations from owning real estate not being used directly in everyday operations and required that the lands be sold to private individuals, not corporations. It also prohibited civil and ecclesiastical corporations from acquiring property in the future. The law of excluded properties allowed the Catholic church to retain its sanctuaries, monasteries, convents, and seminaries. Local state and village governments were allowed to own their offices, jails and schools, but both were forced to sell any other urban and rural real estate.

During the Colonial era the Spanish Crown had granted indigenous communities a certain amount of lands as corporations to ensure that they had sufficient land to maintain their subsistence. Croplands were owned as a corporation in order to discourage sales. Because the lands were deemed corporations, the Lerdo Law forced them to be sold. Individual tenants were given a window of three months in which they had preference of purchase. That system stripped the church of some of its power, but for villagers, enactment of the Lerdo Law amounted to complete confiscation of their lands because individual villagers did not have money to buy land and group ownership required agreement among villagers and made sales a slow and complicated process.

The inequity of forced sales was exacerbated by corrupt judges. When indigenous villagers sought justice from the legal system they were ruled against by judges who were bribed by wealthy Mexicans and by foreigners. The result was development of enormous haciendas combined with a mass of landless peasants who then were hired to work fields they had previously owned.

When Porfirio Diaz came to power in 1876 Mexico was a feudal state with one glorious city at its core; a city which rivaled Paris in sophistication and elegance. Diaz worked to unite the country by building railroads into isolated parts of the country. His goal was to bring a culture based on 14th century feudalism into the 20th century. The goals were admirable but there were unexpected consequences. When farm crops could be transported to world markets the land on which they were grown on became increasingly valuable. The land of the villages was sold at bargain prices. Some haciendas were hundreds of square miles in extension. Fields that once grew corn were planted with sugarcane, a higher priced export crop. Resulting scarcity of corn caused the price of tortillas to rise so that villagers then suffered food shortages.

BIBLIOGRAPHY

Ángeles, Felípe. *Genevevo de la O.*

Atkin, Ronald. *Revolution! Mexico 1910-1920.* New York, John Day Company. 1973.

Bell, Edward I. *The Political Shame of Mexico.* McBride, Nast & Company. New York. 1914.

Beezley, William H. *Insurgent Governor, Abraham Gonzalez and the Mexican Revolution in Chihuahua.* University of Nebraska Press. Lincoln. 1973.

Bonilla, Manuel. *El Régimen Maderista.* Biblioteca de Historia Mexicana. Editorial Arana, México. 1962

Bell, Edward. *The Political Shame of Mexico*, McBride, Nast & Co, New York. 1914.

Bonilla, Manuel Jr., *El Regimen Maderista.* Editorial Arana. México. 1962.

Brenner, Anita. *The Wind That Swept Mexico: The History of the Mexican Revolution.* Austin, University of Texas Press. 1971.

Brunk, Samuel. *Emiliano Zapata!, Revolution & Betrayal in Mexico.* University of New México Press, Albuquerque.1995.

Cervantes, Federico. *Felípe Ángeles en la Revolución.* México. 1964.

Eisenhower, John S.D. *Intervention! The United States and The Mexican Revolution, 1913-1917.* W. W. Norton. New York.1995.

Gilly, Adolfo. *Felípe Ángeles en la Revolución*. Ediciones Era, México. 2008.

__________ *The Mexican Revolution*. The New Press, New York and London. 2005.

Gruening, Ernest, *Mexico and its Heritage*. The Century Co. New York and London, 1928.

Guzman, Martin Luis. *The Eagle and the Serpent*. Translated from the Spanish by Harriet de Onis. Gloucester, Mass. Peter Smith. 1969.

Johnson, William Weber, *Heroic Mexico*. Harcourt Brace Jovanovich, San Diego, New York London. 1984, 1968.

Katz, Friedrich. *The Life & Times of Pancho Villa*. Stanford, CA. Stanford University Press. 1998.

King, Rosa E., *Tempest Over Mexico: A Personal Chronical*. Boston, Little Brown. 1940.

Knight, Alan, *The Mexican Revolution vols. 1 and 2. Counter-Revolution and Reconstruction*. University of Nebraska Press, Lincoln and London. 1986.

Krauze, Enrique Mexico: *Biography of Power, A History of Modern México*, translated by Hank Heifetz. Harper Collins, NY. 1997.

Lloyd, Doloris Huerta. *Crossing the Line*. Book Surge. USA, 2008,

Márquez Sterling, Manuel. *Los Últimos Días del Presidente Madero*. Editorial Porrua. México. 1958.

Matute, Álvaro. *La Revolución Mexicana: Actores, Escenarios, y Acciones*. Oceano. 2009.
Maytorena Papers, Claremont Colleges/Honnold Mudd Library, col no. H19671, Claremont CA.

McCreary, Guy Weddington. *From Glory to Oblivion.* Vantage Press, New York, Washington, Hollywood. 1974.

Meyer, Michael C., Sherman, William L., Deeds Susan M., *The Course of Mexican History.*
Oxford University Press, New York, 1999.

Peuliard, Odile Guilpain, *Felípe Ángeles y los Destinos de la Revolución Mexicana.* Prologo de Adolfo Gilly, Fondo de Cultura Económica. Mexico, D.F.1991.

Schuler, Friedrich E., *Murder and Counterrevolution in Mexico.* University of Nebraska Press. 2015.

Slattery, Matthew. *Felípe Ángeles and the Mexican Revolution.* Prinit Press, Dublin IN. 1974.

Ross, Stanley, *Francisco I. Madero, Apostle of Mexican Democracy.* New York: AMS Press, New York. 1955.

Ruiz, Ramon Edward. *The Great Rebellion, Mexico 1905- 1924.* W.W. Norton, New York, London.1980.

Vasconcelos, José, *Ulises Criollo.* Editoria Trillas. México. 1998.

Wilkie, James W., *Revolution In Mexico.* Alfred A. Knopf, New York. 1969.

[1] Brennen, Anita, *The Wind that Swept Mexico,* University of Texas Press. Austin, Texas. 1971.

[2] Matute, Alvaro. *La Revolucion Mexicana: Actores, Escenarios y Acciones.* Oceano, 2009.

[3] The Sonoran Dynasty : See Appendix.

[4] Peuliard, Odile Guilpain, *Felípe Ángeles y los destinos de la Revolucion Mexicana.* Fondo de Cultura Economica. 1999.

[5] Slattery, Matthew T. Slattery, Felípe Ángeles and the Mexican Revolution, Prinit Press, Dublin, IN. 1969.

[6] Matute, Alvaro. La Revolución Mexicana, Vida Cultual y Politica 1901 – 1929 Oceano. 2009.

[7] Guilpain Peuliard, Odile, *Felípe Ángeles y los destinos de la Revolución Mexicana.* Fondo de Cultura Economica. 1991.

[8] Ibid.

[9] Ross, Stanley, Francisco I. Madero, *Apostle of Mexican Democracy.* AMS Press, New York. 1955. p. 225.

[10] See Appendix: *Plan de Ayala*

[11] Ibíd. 256.

[12] Johnson, William Webber, *Heroic Mexico,* Harcourt Brace Jovanovich, San Diego, London, New York. 1968. p.163.

[13] *ibíd.*

[14] Ángeles, Felípe. *Genovevo de la O.*

[15] Ibid.

[16] King, Rosa E. *Tempest Over Mexico.* Howes Publishing Company, New York, 1944. P.130

[17] Ibid p. 35.

[18] King, Rosa. p. 99.

[19] Ángeles, Felípe, *Genovevo de la O.*

[20] See Appendix: Lerdo Law.

[21] Ángeles, Felípe letter to President Madero.

[22] King, Rosa. p. 99.

[23] Ángeles, Filipe, Genovevo de la O.

[24] Ángeles, Felípe.*Genovevo de la O*

[25] Gilly, Adolfo. *Filipe Ángeles en la Revolución.* 2008.

[26] Ibid.

[27] Ángeles, Felípe, Genovevo de la O.

[28] Ibid.

[29] King, Rosa, Tempest Over Mexico. p.103

[30] Ibid.

[31] Ibid.

[32] Ibid.

[33] Bell, Edward I. *The Political Shame of Mexico*. McBride, Nast & Company, New York. 1914 P. 226.

[34] Bell, Edward I,. *The Political Shame of Mexico and Its Heritage*. McBride, Nast & Co. N.Y. 1914. p. 262.

[35] Ibid.

[36] Greuning, Ernest, *Mexico and Its Heritage*. The Century Co. New York and London. 1928. P. 303.

[37] John, William Webber. *Heroic Mexico*. Harcourt Brace Jovanovich, Publishers, San Diego, NY, London.1968 pp. 99.

[38] Bell. Pp. 270.

[39] Ibid.

[40] Ibid

[41] Ibid.

[42] Ibid

[43] Ibid pp. 278 photo sharpen

[44] Marquez Sterling, Manuel, *Los Ultimos Dias del Presidente Madero,* Editorial Porrua, S.A., Mexico. 1975.

[45] "The bullet which hit Villar was a very choice missile from the cartridge box of fate; the whole clan Madero fell at that shot." Edward I. Bell.

[46] Ibid. pp. 192.

[47] Ibid.

[48] Bonilla, Manuel *El Regimen Maderista,* Biblioteca de Historia Mexicana, Editorial Arana, Mexico 1962.

[49] Marquez Sterling, Manuel, *Los Ultima Dias de Presidente Madero,* Editorial Porrua, Mexico 1975.

[50] Bonilla, pp 167.

[51] King, Rosa. *Tempest Over Mexico.* 111.

[52] King, Rosa. *Tempest Over Mexico.* pp. 107

[53] Ibid

[54] Ibid

[55] Ibid.

[56] Ibid.

[57] Ibid.

[58] Marquez Sterling, M. *Los Ultimnos Dias del Presidente Madero* Editorial Porrua, Mexico, 1975.

[59] Slattery, Matthew. pp. 46.

[60] Marquez Sterling, Manuel. p. 247, 248.

[61] Ibid.

[62] Ross, Stanley R., *Francisco I. Madero, Apostle of Mexican Democracy.* AMS Press, New York, 1955. p. 310.

[63] Schuler, Friedrich E. *Murder & Counterrevolution in Mexico.* University of Nebraska Press, Lincoln and London. 2015. p.49.

[64] Ibid.

[65] Vasconcelos, José, Ulises Criollo, Editoria Trillas, Mexico, 1998 pp. 399-402.

[66] Ross, Stanley R., *Francisco I. Madero, Apostle of Mexican Democracy.* New York: Colombia University Press, 1955, 307-313.

[67] Bonilla, Manuel, *El Regimen Maderista.* Editorial Arana,Mexico. 1922. P.221-223.

[68] Ibid.

[69] Guilpain, Peulliard, Odile. *Felípe Ángeles y los Destinos de la Revolución Mexicana.* Fondo Cultura Económica. Mexico DF, 1991.

[70] Ibíd.

[71] Marquez Sterling, Manuel. *Los Ultimos Dias del Presidente Madero.* Editorial Porrua. Mexico, 1975.

[72] Wilkie, James W. *Revolution in Mexico.* Alfred A. Knopf, New York.1969. pp. 50.

[73] A large room on the second floor of the Palace used for cabinet meetings.

[74] Bonilla. p.223.

[75] Ibid.

[76] Bonilla. 231.

[77] Rurales were militia from villages, a renowned mounted constabulary, not part of the 29th division of Blanquet and Riveroll. See: Ross, R. Stanley, *Francisco I Madero*, AMS Press, NY. 1954.

[78] Slattery. 47.

[79] Ibid.

[80] Ibid.

[81] Huerta to President Taft, February 18, 1913. SDF. 812.00/6256.

[82] Translated from Bonilla, Manuel, *El Regimen Maderista,* Editorial Arana. México 1962. pp 225.

[83] Bonilla, Manuel. Jr. *El Regimen Maderista.* Editorial Arana, México, 1962.

[84] Ibid pp. 83.

[85] McCreary, Guy Weddington, *From Glory to Oblivion* Vantage Press. New York, 1974. pp. 83.

[86] Beezley, William H., *Insurgent Governor, Abraham Gonzalez, and the Mexican Revolution in Chihuahua.* University of Nebraska Press. Lincoln. 1973.

[87] Maytorena Papers. Claremont Colleges/Honnold /Mudd Library, col no.H19671.

[88] McCreary, Guy Weddington. *From Glory to Oblivion,* Vantage Press, N,Y. 1973.

[89] Katz, Friedrich *The Life and Times of Pancho Villa.* Stanford University Press. 1998.

[90] Ibid.

[91] King, Rosa *Tempest Over Mexico,* Howes Publishing Company, 1944. pp.116.

[92] Ibid

[93] Guilpain Peuliard, Odile, *Felípe Ángeles y los Destinos de la Revolución Mexicana.* Fondo de Cultura Economica Mexico, 1991.

[94] Gilly, Adollf.

[95] Cervantes, Federico. *Felípe Ángeles en la Revolucion.* Mexico D.F. 1964.

[96] *Renovadores* were supporters of revolutionary ideals who opposed Madero's methods.

[97] Knight, Alan. *The Mexican Revolution, vol. 2. Counter-revolution and Reconstruction.* University of Nebraska, Lincoln and London, 1990. Pp. 112-115.

[98] Guzman, Martin Luis. *The Eagle and the Serpent.* Doubleday and Co., 1965. Pp. 251.

[99] Ibid.

[100] Lloyd, Doloris Huerta, *Crossing the Line.* BookSurge, USA, 2008.

[101] Ángeles, Felípe, Genovevo de la O.

[102] Katz p. 344.

[103] Ibid.

[104] Ibid. p.147

[105] General Francisco (Pancho) Villa, leader of the Division del Norte.

[106] Following the assassination of President Madero in February of 1913 Felípe Ángeles broke with the federal army and joined the resistance to fight against the

assassin, General Victoriano Huerta. Several of Ángeles admiring students dropped out of military school and went north to join him.

[107] Ángeles is referring to a characteristic action by First Chief of the revolution, Venustiano Carranza was an arrogant man who flaunted his power in petty ways.

[108] Major Ángeles was the general's younger brother. SEH

[109] Womack John Jr., *Zapata and the Mexican Revolution,* New York: Vintage Books, 400-404. 1968.